IMAGES
of America

AFRICAN AMERICANS
IN SEWICKLEY VALLEY

H. W. Blockson and Son Hauling. Hauling and moving was among the easier businesses to get into, as all that was needed was a horse and a wagon. Advertisements like this helped to get the word out for H. W. Blockson and Son Hauling. Of all Sewickley's black businesses, H. W. Blockson and Son Hauling was among the largest and longest standing. Founded in 1907, the company moved into the hands of Ellis Blockson upon his father's death in 1919. When Ellis married Susan Jason, she became an asset to the administrative and financial details of the business. In 1950, the business was sold to blacks James and Francis Powell, who maintained the company, with its name, until they sold it in 1971.

On the cover: **Ellis Blockson and His First Truck.** The first H. W. Blockson and Son Hauling truck was an Indiana purchased around 1916 by Horace Blockson's son, Ellis. Until he bought this truck, the owner had never driven a motorized vehicle, but upon its purchase, without hesitation (or tests), he made an application, paid a fee, and was issued his driver's license. The truck operated primarily in the Sewickley area, but there were no state, federal, or labor regulations, so it also traveled widely in tristate counties and made a few trips to eastern Pennsylvania, New York State, Delaware, and Maryland. (Courtesy of Bettie Cole, from the files of Susan Blockson.)

IMAGES
of America

AFRICAN AMERICANS IN SEWICKLEY VALLEY

Bettie Cole and Autumn Redcross

ARCADIA
PUBLISHING

Published by Arcadia Publishing
Charleston SC, Chicago IL, Portsmouth NH, San Francisco CA

Printed in the United States of America

Library of Congress Catalog Card Number: 2008921891

For all general information contact Arcadia Publishing at:
Telephone 843-853-2070
Fax 843-853-0044
E-mail sales@arcadiapublishing.com
For customer service and orders:
Toll-Free 1-888-313-2665

Visit us on the Internet at www.arcadiapublishing.com

SUSAN BLOCKSON. Susan Blockson, a prominent African American lady, wife to Ellis Blockson of H. W. Blockson and Son Hauling, and the Sewickley community's acknowledged authority on local black history, remained active in this community until age and fragility overcame her outwardly. Her memory remains largely in the movement to continue preservation and documentation of the history of African Americans in Sewickley. This book is dedicated to all the men, women, and children whose lives are a part of this photographic collection, and whose families have been gracious enough to share that gift, and to all memory keepers such as Susan Blockson, without whom there would be no account.

CONTENTS

ACKNOWLEDGMENTS

Please accept our gratitude without limits to all who assisted in the completion of this project, including the Antioch Freewill Baptist Church, St. Matthews African Methodist Episcopal Zion Church, Triumph Baptist Church, Daniel B. Matthews Historical Society, Quaker Valley Public School District, the Sewickley Public Library, the Sewickley Valley Hospital, the Sewickley Valley Historical Society, Julia Elizabeth Addison, Beverlee Blair, Mattie King Butler, Chiquita Clark, Daisy Crawford, Rev. Charles Drinkard Jr., Albert and Alegra Frank, Rev. Lee Haney, Sarah Harris, Karen Henderson, Grace and Murch King, Evelyn Lee, Felton Martin, Susan Morris, Leslie Bobonis Myers, Mildred Nash, Eliza Nevin, Constance Pickett, Ann Rideout, Thomas Robertson, Arlene Rucker, William Rucker, Donna, Lawson, and Evelyn Shaw, Dorinda Taylor, Kenneth and Melunsena Whitlock, Russ Williams, Shirley Wormsley, and Helene Zacharias.

In the spirit of James Addison, who served this community tirelessly as a photographer and friend, this project serves as a glimpse into the lives of blacks in Sewickley Valley. All photographs, unless otherwise noted, are part of the collection of Bettie Cole and the files of Susan Blockson. For a detailed account and history, please refer to Bettie Cole's work, *Their Story: The History of Blacks/African Americans in Sewickley and Edgeworth*.

INTRODUCTION

While Pittsburgh was being established as an industrial and financial stronghold in the nation, 14 miles west of downtown a quintessential American village was born in the valley called Sewickley, named by the Shawnees and Iroquois. The new American government had designated the land to pay Revolutionary War soldiers upon the depreciation of the continental currency. The land was surveyed and divided as European and American settlers began to build there.

Formerly a Native American trail, Sewickley developed as a pastoral village along Beaver Road and became a major thoroughfare between Pittsburgh and the Northwest Territory. Soon wealthy Pittsburghers were building summer and year-round homes in the Sewickley Valley—set apart from the hustle and pollution of town. With them they brought the first African Americans to make Sewickley Valley their home.

History records that Jim Robinson was the first black man to come and make his home in Sewickley Bottom. Robinson, a servant in the Shields household, came with the family from its Washington County plantation to its landholdings in Edgeworth. History persuades that Jim Robinson was given his freedom through the transition, as settlers across the Ohio River often thought they were in Virginia.

Early black settlers and some passing through the valley made their way to Sewickley Bottom via the Underground Railroad. The community, made up largely of Quakers and abolitionists sympathetic to their cause, offered safe houses and provisions to those when able. Establishments and private families would emerge as stations and conductors on the route to freedom, with the Ohio River giving a promising passage.

Known as Sewickley's early African American pioneers, some who came to stay are recorded in history as William Blakenship, Charles "Pop" Reese, Pete Davis, George Marlatt, Thomas Branson, Israel Jackson, Albert Fields, David Brooks, Dennis Buchannan, William "Pap" Fischer, James Parker, Benjamin Ford, Philip Brown, John C. Howard, Franklin Whets, Mary Jackson, William Curtis, John Ward, John Pryor, William Anderson, William and Sarah Jane Henderson, Lucy and Jesse Carter, Rev. Daniel B. Matthews and Rev. Billie Fleming, and William Warfield.

These men and women would work largely as domestics for private families and in construction as teamsters as Sewickley's area flourished. A second wave of black settlers would come during the World War I period because of the need for mill workers. Increasingly black men and women and their families would settle in the area and make it their home.

As early as 1857, Sewickley's first black mission would emerge when Daniel B. Matthews, a circuit minister, came to the valley from Philadelphia. Church meetings and services would be held in area cabins, in parks, and in the homes of one another. Ultimately five predominantly black churches would be born: St. Matthews African Methodist Episcopal Zion Church, St. John's African Methodist Episcopal Zion Church (1884–1920), Antioch Freewill Baptist Church (organized in 1890), Triumph Baptist Church (founded in 1905), and the Antioch Fire Baptized Holiness Church (1916–1979). From the early days, they would not only represent the center of religious activity but social events as well. It was the churches that initiated first dinners, lawn fetes, ice-cream socials, plays, and pageants. The church often was the only and most likely place to hold various community club meetings and gatherings.

Later opportunity in Sewickley enabled blacks to open their own businesses, such as blacksmiths, barbers, and store proprietors. Talents and skills emerged from the black community in all areas, including shoe shining, taxi driving, cooking and catering, and sewing, and more would find their skills and talents providing them with their livelihood as well.

For outdoor recreation and events, blacks gathered at White's field for baseball picnics and summer holiday festivities. Located between the railroad tracks and Chadwick Street, White's field was in close proximity to what would soon become the "Y-Field."

The Colored YMCA was the first major milestone in the black recreational and social history in the Sewickley Valley. Blacks were not allowed to go to the white YMCA, so in 1913, they organized their own in St. Matthews African Methodist Episcopal Zion's old building on Walnut Street. The Walnut Street Y (as it became known as) remained a strong and active organization for the black community until a great storm in June 1924 flooded the basement and undermined its foundation. For many years, the YMCA struggled, operating from nonpermanent headquarters, and the Colored YMCA steadily declined.

The Sewickley Colored Community Center succeeded the Colored YMCA in serving the black community. A group of local black men known as the Young Men's Club and the Sewickley Ministerial Association organized the Sewickley Colored Community Center during the mid- to late 1930s. In March 1939, the center received its charter and in 1943 became a member of the Community Chest of Allegheny County (now known as the United Way of Allegheny County).

The Sewickley Public School Pavilion and the Chadwick Street field were two other facilities that served the black community. The pavilion was used for basketball, volleyball, summer camp programs, and proms. The YMCA used the pavilion for many of its functions, as did the Sewickley Colored Community Center, until the latter added its gymnasium to its new building.

The center's first headquarters consisted of two small buildings on Division Street between Broad Street and Locust Place. Rapidly growing out of these headquarters, the center moved in 1951 to its present Chadwick Street location. Giant strides were made on Chadwick Street with an ever-growing agenda of programming and activity. Renovations to the building diversified athletic options, including the donation of the adjacent field, newly built tennis courts, and eventually an outdoor swimming pool with adjoining kiddie pool.

Having black servicemen of the Sewickley Valley participate in each of the wars, Walter Robinson American Legion Post 450 serves as a memorial to their service given. It was organized in September 1922 at the Walnut Street YMCA. First meeting from house to house and then sustaining location at a few buildings, Post 450 found a home in the Sewickley's old train station that was moved from then Rail Road Avenue (at the foot of Broad Street) to Chadwick Street when the tracks were moved back to accommodate a road for increasing motor vehicle activity.

Conveniently located across from the community center's new building and field, Post 450 and the community center would together create a culturally rich environment for the black community. Added to Post 450 was a pavilion, which ushered in the era of the big band. Hosting such talents as Duke Ellington, Ella Fitzgerald, Dizzy Gillespie, and Cab Calloway, the post would become a draw for jazz lovers from all around. Known to be the largest facility in the village, other events would fall into Post 450's pavilion, including the March of Dimes annual ball, the annual Christmas party put on by both the post and the Sewickley Community Center, harvest festivals, proms, and ladies' teas.

With the changing of times and the loosening of social dynamics, the influences that made Sewickley's black dynamic community are no longer seen as a necessity today. But their story remains. And what the village is today is because of what was done yesterday. This project aims to give tribute and a glimpse of the lives and times of the African Americans of Sewickley Valley.

One

THEY CAME TO WORK

SEWICKLEY, FROM ANDERSON'S HILL.

OVERLOOKING SEWICKLEY VALLEY. Sewickley Valley has always had an appeal for the African American. Early settlers would come to live among Quakers, abolitionists, and members of the community sympathetic to the cause of freedom and the rights of men. The first black mission (which later became St. Matthews African Methodist Episcopal Zion Church) developed the reputation as a station for those black men and women fleeing for their freedom by way of the Underground Railroad. Early in the 19th century, blacks began to settle the area. They came to work as domestics, teamsters, and construction workers. Some bought property and opened their own shops and businesses, making a home for themselves. Giving way to succeeding generations, African Americans continue to be a strong part of the community in the Sewickley Valley. (Courtesy of *Lights and Shadows of Sewickley Life.*)

"Ma" Davis. Stories of flights for freedom resound through the village as Quakers, abolitionists, and members of the community sentimental to the cause of freedom were said to provide safe houses for those running from the plight of enslavement. The Davis Homestead was one such station known to shelter people within its cellar and pump house. Eliza Cochran Davis, known affectionately as "Ma" Davis, told her children and grandchildren that one of her talents in life was her ability to teach people, all people, to read so that they could know the Bible. (Courtesy of the Sewickley Valley Historical Society.)

The Ohio River. As the Mississippi River's largest tributary, the Ohio River proved a natural route from slavery to freedom; enslaved men and women would smuggle among the freight aboard steamboats at Louisville. When the more hospitable shores of Pennsylvania were reached, the Ohio River provided an ideal route from Pittsburgh to Beaver County for fugitives fleeing by way of the Underground Railroad. As early as 1809, a road linking these two localities provided means for overland transport. (Courtesy of the Sewickley Valley Historical Society.)

CAPT. DAVID SHIELDS PROPERTY. Early pioneer Jim Robinson is reportedly the first black man to have come to Sewickley Valley. It is recorded that he came as early as 1823, brought as a servant and presumably freed man with Capt. David Shields when he moved from Washington County to his family holdings in Sewickley. The Daniel B. Matthews Historical Society sponsored a bus tour that included the Shields homestead pictured here.

WILLIAM P. FORD AND FAMILY. William P. Ford is the descendant of Benjamin and Lucy Ford, who lived on the Shields property along Beaver Road near Little Sewickley Creek. William P. Ford was a horseman and a chauffeur working for the Alexander Laughlin family for years.

THE PARKER FAMILY. Early African American pioneer families who resided in Sewickley were employed as domestics in private families. Pictured here is the family of James Parker at their home on the knoll at the foot of Sand Hill, the estate of their employer, squire John Way Jr. and family. Brothers George and Bill Parker display their instrumental interests on the zither and banjo. George, with the zither, worked the Way family kitchen and waited tables while Bill, on the banjo, tended the horses.

PENNSYLVANIA LINES WEST OF PITTSBURGH.
PENNSYLVANIA COMPANY—EASTERN DIVISION.
OFFICE OF THE SUPERINTENDENT.
ALLEGHENY, PA.

Allegheny,Pa.,Oct.5th,1901.

Edw. Aston,

Dear Sir:-

I hand you ___ with a piece of the drapery used on Engine No.66 on President McKinley's funeral train,September 18th,1901.

Kindly accept it as a memento of the occasion and with my compliments.

Yours truly,

A. M. Schoyer,
Superintendent.

EDWARD ASTON. Working for the Pennsylvania Rail West, Edward Aston's performance was so convincing that superintendent A. M. Schoyer gave him a part of engine No. 66's fabric draping from the funeral train of the late president William McKinley.

THE ELMHURST INN. The Elmhurst Inn and the Park Place Hotel were two posh lodgings that helped to establish Sewickley as a choice summer colony in the first part of the 20th century. African American pioneers of the valley found work in these establishments as chefs and waiters. The Sewickley Country Inn at Boundary Street and Ohio River Boulevard now stands where the Elmhurst Inn had been. The Park Place Hotel was located at the foot of Broad Street and what is now Ohio River Boulevard. Both establishments were convenient to reach from the Sewickley train station. (Courtesy of the Sewickley Valley Historical Society.)

13

D. W. CHALLIS CONSTRUCTION COMPANY. Many folks are said to have come from Kentucky to work for the D. W. Challis Construction Company in Sewickley Valley. Without a fear of hard

work, African Americans found jobs with willing employers such as Challis. (Courtesy of the Sewickley Valley Historical Society.)

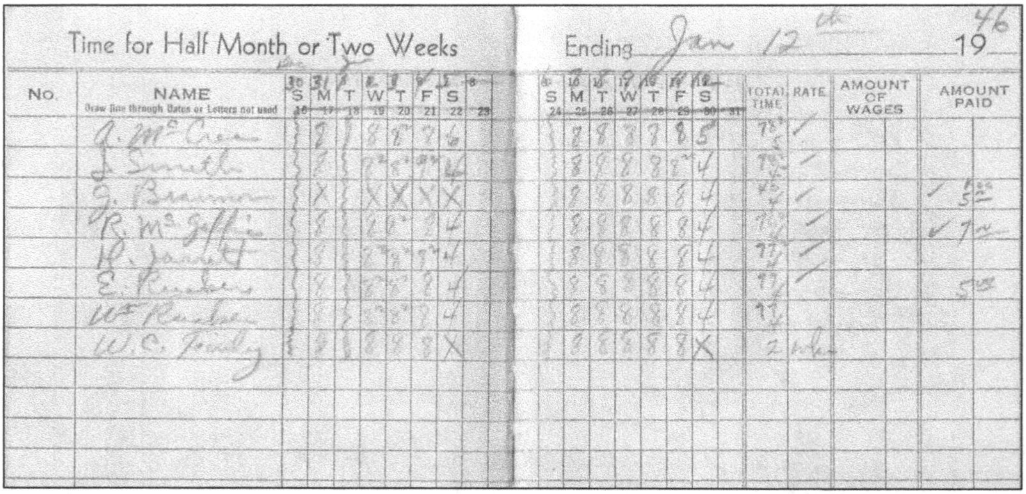

Time for Half Month or Two Weeks — Ending Jan 12th 1946

No.	NAME (Draw line through Dates or Letters not used)	S	M	T	W	T	F	S	S	M	T	W	T	F	S	TOTAL TIME	RATE	AMOUNT OF WAGES	AMOUNT PAID

CHALLIS CONSTRUCTION PAY BOOK. Generations of black men and their children would work within the same trade. William "Witt" Rucker, following in the footsteps of his father, would also work for D. W. Challis Construction Company. Following his service in the war, Rucker began his tenure with Challis through its transition to Kean and Wise Construction in 1946 and then to Wise Construction in 1953. Rucker worked as a truck driver, a laborer, and then a maintenance man from 1945 until he retired in 1996. (Courtesy of William Rucker.)

WILLIAM RUCKER AND HIS TEAM OF HORSES. Shown here is William Rucker, a Sewickley native born in March 1922. Having grown up watching his father work as a teamster with the Challis organization, raising ponies came naturally to him. At age seven, he watched his father use a horse-drawn dump wagon to create the roads during the week and a plow on the fields on the weekend. Rucker purchased his first team after returning home from World War II. (Courtesy of William Rucker.)

SEWICKLEY VETERINARY ADVERTISEMENT. This advertisement included in the book *Lights and Shadows of Sewickley Life* depicts black men working with horses and presumably other farm animals for a local veterinarian. (Courtesy of *Lights and Shadows of Sewickley Life.*)

MCPHERSON BROTHERS CONSTRUCTION COMPANY TEAMSTERS. McPherson Brothers of Edgeworth was another construction company heavily staffed by African Americans. The main employment for black men was as domestics, teamsters, chauffeurs, and deliverymen through the years by horse and wagon and then trucks and vans. (Courtesy of the Sewickley Valley Historical Society.)

HEGNER'S EMPORIUM IN CONSTRUCTION. As seen here, African Americans worked alongside whites during construction. Here they make up part of the workforce hired to build for George Hegner, proprietor of Hegner's Emporium. (Courtesy of the Sewickley Valley Historical Society.)

HEGNER'S EMPORIUM. African American Howard Brown Sr. worked for Hegner's most of his life. His duties and tasks were varied and included delivery by horse and wagon, and later trucks and vans, work as a janitor, and sometimes even work as a sales clerk. (Courtesy of the Sewickley Valley Historical Society.)

THE KING FAMILY. Matthew King and his young family came from Coraopolis to Sewickley with his employer John Bell. Working as the butler and chauffeur to John Bell, Matthew King would move his family first to Diggs' Apartment Building on Nevin Avenue before purchasing their family house on Centennial Street. (Courtesy of Mattie King Butler.)

SEWICKLEY VALLEY HOSPITAL WORKERS. The Sewickley Valley Hospital was the largest employer of blacks in Sewickley Valley. On July 20, 1907, the Sewickley hospital had its formal opening, and it was enlarged in 1909. In this picture, a young Mattie King poses with an unidentified hospital worker on her left and Alan Anderson, longtime hospital employee, on her right. (Courtesy of Mattie King Butler.)

TEMORA HAYNES AND MATTIE BRAXTON. Pictured here are two of Sewickley's eldest residents, Temora Haynes (August 1890–October 1995) and Mattie Braxton (September 1885–May 1992). Together they celebrate their status as centenarians. Early pioneers of this village, they worked as domestics for families such as the Applegates and the Chapmans. They were photographed in 1991 by Clif Page for the *Allegheny Times* and *Beaver County Times*.

JAMES G. MATTHEWS. Pictured here is James G. Matthews, the grandson of Rev. Daniel B. Matthews, who founded and led the first black mission in Sewickley Valley, which later became the St. Matthews African Methodist Episcopal Zion Church on Thorn and Walnut Streets. (Courtesy of the Sewickley Herald.)

Two

WORSHIP CAME FIRST

| J. H. Holmes Supply | E. L. Green Triumph Baptist (now transferred) | Moses Taylor Supply | James Ford Church of God Coraopolis | G. E. Sallie Antioch Baptist Church | M. S. Rudd St. Matthew's A. M. E. Zion Chur |

All photographs on this page are by Harry Reno

SEWICKLEY'S AFRICAN AMERICAN CHURCH LEADERS. At one time in Sewickley there were five predominantly black congregations. Still meeting are St. Matthews African Methodist Episcopal Zion Church located on Thorn and Walnut Streets and organized in 1853; Antioch Freewill Baptist Church located on Elizabeth Street and organized in 1890; and the Triumph Baptist Church located on Ferry and Frederick Streets and organized in 1905. No longer meeting are the St. John's African Methodist Episcopal Zion Church (1884–late 1920s) and the Antioch Fire Baptized Holiness Church (1916–1979). Familiar church leaders shown in this clipping include Rev. E. L. Green of Triumph, Rev. G. E. Sallie of Antioch, and Rev. M. S. Rudd of St. Matthews African Methodist Episcopal Zion Church. (Courtesy of the Sewickley Valley Historical Society.)

Four Generations of The Matthews Family

Great-Grandmother . . .
Mrs. Catherine Matthews, 1834-1914
Widow of Rev. Daniel Matthews
Founder of St. Matthew's Church

Grandfather . . . .
James D. Matthews, 1856-1933
Secretary of Trustee Board

Father . . .
James G. Matthews
Present Treasurer, Trustee Board

Infant . . .
Helen Elizabeth Matthews
Now Mrs. Archie Ball
of Los Angeles, California

DANIEL B. MATTHEWS FAMILY GENERATION PHOTOGRAPH. This 110th anniversary bulletin image depicts four generations of the founder Rev. Daniel B. Matthews's family. Shown seated are his widow, Catherine Matthews, and their son James D. Matthews, standing is the grandson James G. Matthews, and in his hands is his daughter Helen Elizabeth. The six charter members are recorded as John Howard and wife, M. Jones and wife, Franklin Whets, and Miss Hamilton. (Courtesy of St. Matthews African Methodist Episcopal Zion Church.)

SEWICKLEY'S FIRST BLACK MISSION. The first black mission that attracted African American believers throughout Sewickley Valley was founded in April 1857 by Rev. Daniel B. Matthews, a circuit clergyman of the African Methodist Episcopal Conference in Philadelphia. Before the mission was established on the corner of Walnut and Thorn Streets, meetings were held in family homes and log cabins and in close-by parks and groves. These parks and groves were also sites for church camp meetings, revivals, lawn fetes, and picnics. The mission would later become the St. Matthews African Methodist Episcopal Zion Church when the property at Thorn and Walnut Streets was purchased and the church's first building was erected.

22

BURNING OF THE MORTGAGE, 1917.
St. Matthews African Methodist Episcopal
Zion Church's new building was dedicated on
Sunday, March 3, 1912. Five years later in 1917
and during the ministry of Rev. O. J. Ramsen,
the mortgage was burned. (Courtesy of the
Sewickley Valley Historical Society.)

COME AND HELP US

GRAND RALLY TO PAY OFF MORTGAGE AT

ST. MATTHEW'S A. M. E. ZION CHURCH
Corner Thorn and Walnut Streets, Sewickley, Pa.

Sunday, June 10, 1917

One of the scholars of our race, in the person of Rev. E.
D. W. Jones, A.M., D.D., of Rochester, N. Y., will preach
at 10.45 a. m. and 8.00 p. m.
At 3.00 p. m. Rev. W. D. Clinton, M.D., of Carnegie,
Pa., will preach.

The following will assist during the day:

Rev. J. R. Walters, of Coraopolis, Pa.; Rev. H. S. Hicks,
of West Bridgewater, Pa.; Rev. S. A. Johnson, of Triumph
Baptist Church; Rev. C. Henry, of Antioch Baptist Church;
Mrs. A. Addison, of St. John's A. M. E. Church.

SPECIAL MUSIC WILL BE RENDERED BY CHOIR

SO THAT YOU CAN STAY ALL DAY:
Dinner will be served from 12.00 m. to 1.00 p. m.—25c.
Supper will be served from 6.00 to 7.00 p. m.—15c.
The high cost of living hinders us from giving it away.

AT ST. MATTHEW'S A. M. E. ZION CHURCH

On Monday, June 11, 1917, at 8:30 P. M.
Rev. E. D. W. Jones, A.M., D.D., Will Lecture. Subject:
"Our Race in the Past, Present and Future"
Admission 15 cents

JAS. REESE, Church Clerk   O. J. REMSEN, Pastor

ST. MATTHEWS AFRICAN METHODIST EPISCOPAL ZION CHURCH. The current church facade
was erected and then dedicated on March 3, 1912. The old frame church was moved from the
corner to a location next door facing Walnut Street. A small frame house was donated and
moved from George Christy's property to Thorn Street to become the St. Matthews parsonage.
(Courtesy of St. Matthews African Methodist Episcopal Zion Church.)

EASTER SUNDAY, 1937. The youth of the church had many participatory options. There was a Pansies group, a Buds of Promise club, and a Sunday school circus to help minister to the children of the church. Among the St. Matthews "church pillars" were Leona Calloway and her husband, Charles. Leona participated devotedly in the varied youth ministries of the church as well as held roles as missionary secretary and special program chairperson of the Progressive Tea. She also was a member of the Hawthorne Club. (Courtesy of St. Matthews African Methodist Episcopal Zion Church.)

JAMES VARRICK MEN'S GROUP. Named for one of the founders of Zion Methodism and African Methodist Episcopal Zion's first bishop, the James Varrick Men's Group took an active part in the church's annual men's day and in May 1965 donated the impressive outdoor bulletin board to announce church services and events. The group was organized under the ministry of Rev. Eugene Morgan. (Courtesy of St. Matthews African Methodist Episcopal Zion Church.)

ST. MATTHEWS AFRICAN METHODIST EPISCOPAL ZION CHURCH, 1967. The full congregation of the church stands on its steps in 1967 in celebration of the 110th anniversary. (Courtesy of St. Matthews African Methodist Episcopal Zion Church.)

ST. MATTHEWS AFRICAN METHODIST EPISCOPAL ZION CHURCH, HISTORIC LANDMARK.
As a result of the efforts of a committee of church members, led my Melunsena Whitlock,
St. Matthews African Methodist Episcopal Zion Church was designated as a historic landmark
in August 1997 by the Pittsburgh History and Landmarks Foundation. (Courtesy of Kenneth
and Melunsena Whitlock.)

ST. MATTHEWS CONGREGATION, 1997. Shown here is the congregation photograph taken on the
steps of St. Matthews African Methodist Episcopal Zion Church in the fall of 1997, Rev. Zedric
Coaston presiding. (Courtesy of St. Matthews African Methodist Episcopal Zion Church.)

PASTOR DRINKARD JR. Following a lineage of dedicated pastors over the last century and a half, Rev. Charles Drinkard Jr. has come to lead the family at St. Matthews African Methodist Episcopal Zion. Seated in front of Reverend Drinkard is church mother Dorothy Aston Butler. Deaconesses standing in white include Laura Brannon, Daisy Crawford, Inez Jarret, Janice Patillo, Arlene Rucker, Constance Pickett, and local preacher Tawana Seals. Choir members shown are Alan Milliner, Thomas "Scoby" Robertson, Gloria "Peaches" Cook, Ulysses "Mike" Hannon, Nancy Seals, Marie Hannon, Marilyn Crump, and pianist Grace Cherry King. Devoted members shown include Henry Scales, Sally Smith, Joyce Parker, Melunsena Whitlock, Ceola Patillo, Murch King, Tazmirah (Taz) Quesinberry, Kenneth Whitlock, Zoey Cook, Viki Rideout, Shonte Cook, Walter Brannon, and general officer Helene Zacharias. (Courtesy of St. Matthews African Methodist Episcopal Zion Church.)

ANTIOCH FREEWILL BAPTIST CHURCH. The Antioch Freewill Baptist Church was organized in 1890 with the leadership of Rev. C. W. Frazer. In 1906, Rev. John Kirk became pastor and remained until his untimely death in 1909 at the age of 54. In 1915, Antioch received its official charter with named members Eli Bowler, Solomon Toliver, J. H. Jones, James Ford, Harry Kirk, William Gains, George Lee, and George Thomas. Its original storefront building on Division Street was lost by fire.

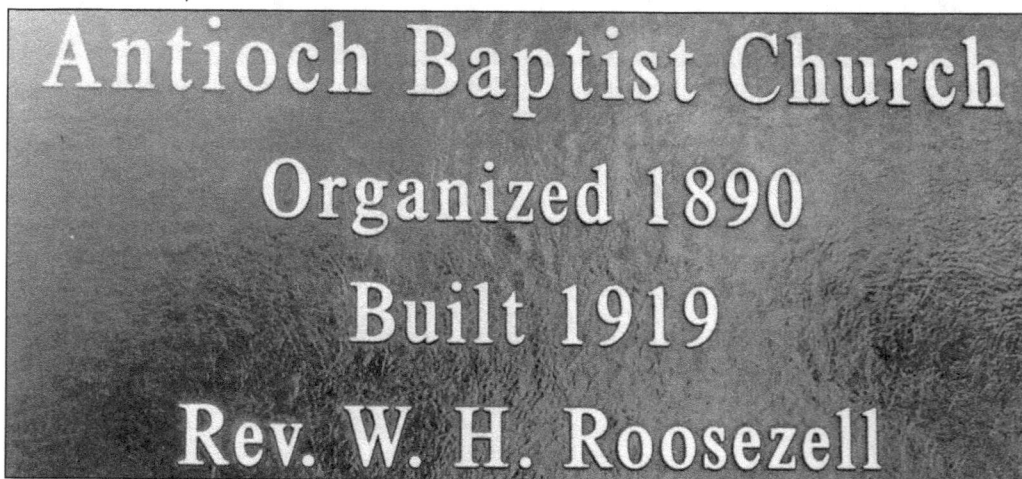

ANTIOCH PLAQUE. Soon after losing the original building to fire, Antioch purchased the land where the church stands today. On this land, the church initially operated out of two houses—one used for church services and the other as the parsonage. Antioch's present place of worship was built under the leadership of Rev. W. H. Roosezell in 1918. Men who have served Antioch Freewill Baptist as ministers include Rev. C. W. Frazer, Rev. John Kirk, Reverend Roosezell, Reverend Mason, Rev. G. E. Sallie, Reverend Roberts, Rev. E. M. Brown, Reverend Battles, Rev. O. R. Tipper, Rev. Albert Gans, Reverend Langhorne, Rev. Ronald Glenn, Reverend Massey, Rev. Donald Smith, Rev. Norman Hunt, and Rev. Troy Sligh. (Courtesy of Antioch Freewill Baptist Church.)

A TOM THUMB WEDDING. Mark Frank of Antioch Freewill Baptist Church officiates at a Tom Thumb wedding ceremony for the beaming bridal party. From left to right are Stephanie Smith, unidentified, Andres Farrington, Kathleen Frank, Craig Whitlock, and Steven Boswell. (Courtesy of the Sewickley Herald and the family of James Addison.)

MINISTRY AT ANTIOCH. As with each of the other churches, the youth ministry and the music ministry are a vital and integral part of the congregation. Junior ushers in white pose for a photograph with Rev. Ronald Glenn, who pastored Antioch between 1976 and 1984. Below, Hosea Banks, daughter of Deacon Herbert and Nellie Proctor and longtime pianist of Antioch Freewill Baptist Church, plays enthusiastically for the congregation and guests. (Above, courtesy of Antioch Freewill Baptist Church.)

ANTIOCH ALL. Senior members Lorena Adams and Ida Harrison, seated in the church sanctuary, are longtime members of Antioch. Below, Antioch youth prepare to participate in Sewickley's bicentennial parade. In that year, Antioch Freewill Baptist Church celebrated its 113th anniversary. Antioch's current deacons are Lorenzo Adams, Albert Frank, and Samuel Smith. Church deaconesses are Katrina Adams, Tammy Burke, Carol Cafrelli, Alegra Frank, Shamina Frank, Mary Gandy, and Charmayne Smith. The church continues to thrive under the leadership of Minister Jerome Johnson, Minister Richard Owens, and Rev. Troy Sligh. (Courtesy of Antioch Freewill Baptist Church.)

TRIUMPH BAPTIST CHURCH. In December 1904, several individuals met at the residence of Charles Anderson and his wife for the purpose of organizing a missionary Baptist church. What resulted was the organization of the Triumph Baptist Church on June 14, 1905, with the leadership of pastors and laymen from the Allegheny General Baptist Association. Meetings continued in the home of the Andersons, until a small frame building was erected on leased property on Centennial Avenue. In 1908, property was purchased at the corner of Frederick and Ferry Streets, and a new small frame building went up in 1911. Services continued there, even as the present edifice was being built around it in 1924. At the completion of the new building, the former building within it was demolished. Triumph charter members are Mr. and Mrs. Creed Smith, Mr. and Mrs. Robert Maze, Mr. and Mrs. Ellis A. Williams, Mollie Burrell, and Mr. and Mrs. Charles Anderson.

Rev. R.B. Cobbs* 1908-1913

Rev. William Moore* 1913-1914

Rev. Emmet L. Green* 1922-1940

Rev. James L. Moore 1941-1945

Rev. Finis H. Austin 1946-1950

Rev. Emory Taylor 1952-1953

TRIUMPH PAST PASTORS. Former pastors of Triumph include Rev. E. N. Johnson, Reverend Young, Rev. R. B. Cobbs, Rev. S. A. Johnson, Rev. William Moore, Rev. Emmet L. Green, Rev. James L. Moore, Rev. Finis H. Austin, Rev. Emory Taylor, Rev. Matthew L. Daw, Rev. Samuel L. White, and Rev. Jezreel Toliver.

Rev. Matthew L. Daw 1955-1962

Rev. Samuel L. White 1963-1969

REVEREND JEZREEL TOLIVER

FORMER PASTORS.
Pastors not pictured are Triumph's first, second, and fourth pastors, Rev. E. N. Johnson, Reverend Young, and Rev. S. A. Johnson. Currently Triumph's associate pastors include Rev. Lee Haney, Rev. Lafayette Vance, Rev. Fred Catalano, Rev. Glenn Loper, Rev. Geneva Short, Minister Donna Jones, Minister Kim Booker, and Minister Lee Haney Jr.

Triumph Baptist Church Congregation taken around 1935
Rev. E. L. Green's Pastorate

Triumph Baptist Church Congregation April 1980
Rev. Jezreel Toliver's Pastorate

TRIUMPH BAPTIST CHURCH CONGREGATION. Appearing in the 75th anniversary booklet are two Triumph Baptist congregational photographs. The first is under the pastorate of Rev. Emmet L. Green, and the second was taken under the pastorate of Rev. Jezreel Toliver in April 1980.

REV. C. L. GILES. Rev. C. L. Giles has lovingly pastored Triumph Baptist Church for 20 years. Triumph's current deacon board consists of chairman Jim Jackson, Edward Hollins, Keith Davis, Leo Clements, Melvin Steals Jr., and Arthur Woods. The church trustees are chairman Greg Haus, Carlos Carter, Robert Lewis, Robert Liggett, Evelyn Lee, Lois Rush, Gloria Johnson, Simquita Bridges, Alvin Carter, Donald Bryant, Vincent Johnson, Joe Simms, Eric Dunn, and Eric Blair. (Courtesy of the family of James Addison.)

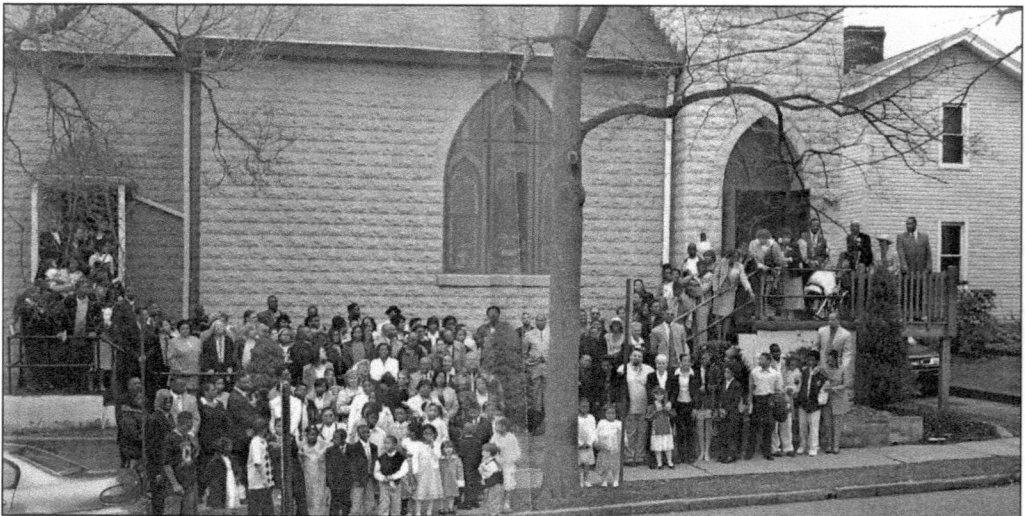

TRIUMPH BAPTIST CHURCH CONGREGATION. This congregational photograph was taken in celebration of the church's 100th anniversary in 2005. At present, Triumph has secured a new location and is making plans to build a larger church to accommodate its growing congregation.

CHURCH LADIES. The women pictured for some yet unknown occasion represent the three predominantly black congregations in Sewickley, which illustrates the church community's connectivity. From left to right are (first row) Sarah Ogletree, Hattie Clay, Rachel Brown of St. Matthews, and Pheobe Gibson; (second row) Ethel Randolph of Triumph, Dorothy Blair of Antioch, Louise Jenkins of St. Matthews, and Mildred Grey and Helen Tucker of Triumph Baptist Church. (Courtesy of St. Matthews African Methodist Episcopal Zion Church.)

ST. JOHN'S AFRICAN METHODIST EPISCOPAL ZION SUPPORTERS. When William Anderson Sr. bought his family home on 14 Elizabeth Street, he also purchased and owned the property next door for the small St. John's African Methodist Episcopal Zion Church building and its parsonage located behind the church. William Anderson Sr. was one of the pioneer members of St. John's. Both he and his son William S. Anderson Jr. were faithful and active members. Dedicated on August 3, 1884, the church remained on the Anderson property until it disbanded around the late 1920s. Pictured here are William S. Anderson Jr., his wife, Mabel, and their son James (Jimmy).

ANTIOCH FIRE BAPTIZED HOLINESS CHURCH. The Antioch Fire Baptized Holiness Church was organized in 1916, and Sewickley resident Moses Fisher Sr. was synonymous with the Holiness Church, having, at one time, served as its minister and remaining a staunch and dedicated member until the church disbanded in 1979. After first meeting in homes, and then in the old disbanded St. John's African Methodist Episcopal Zion Church building, the tiny congregation moved to a small one-room frame building on Walnut Street that it purchased in 1933. It was reported that brother Moses Fisher Sr., pictured here, practically rebuilt the building to suit the purposes for the church. Having one time served as its minister, Moses Fisher Sr. remained a staunch and dedicated member until the church disbanded in 1979.

Three

BUSINESS AND LIVELIHOOD

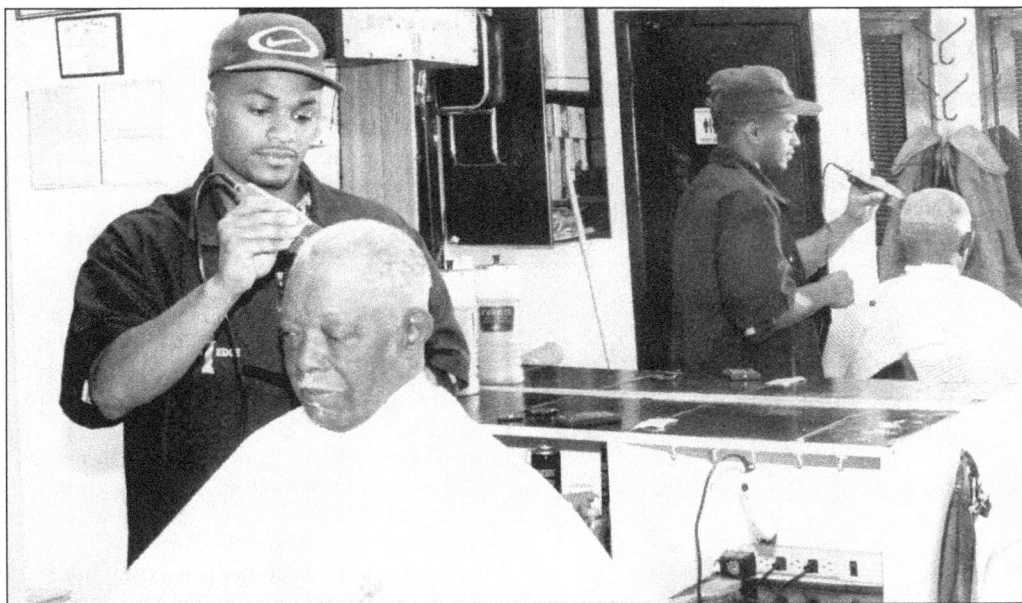

AN OLD AND NEW BUSINESS. Through the years, African Americans in Sewickley would turn to their own talents, skills, and entrepreneurship to provide their family's income through a business of their own. A variety of services and products could be gained from black businesses beginning before the dawn of the 20th century. Sewickley's first documented businesses operated by black men were two separate barbershops, one operated by John "Pop" Howard and the other by the Fleming brothers, around 1885 or earlier. The Fleming brothers' shop was on Broad Street by Wolcott Park. John Howard's shop included a small confectionary store and was located on Chestnut Street and the railroad (now Ohio River Boulevard). However, John Howard and the Fleming brothers cut only the hair of white men in their shops. Down through the years, there have been many barbershops in the valley owned and operated by African Americans. Carlos Norman continues this tradition as he owns and operates the Cuttin Edge barbershop on Locust Street, originally built by Lewis Hampton in 1963.

BUTLER'S VALLEY CATERING COMPANY. John D. Butler came to Sewickley in 1890. While working as a chef at one of the local hotels, he soon became an entrepreneur, founding the Butler Brothers ice-cream store and caterer, also known as Valley Butler Catering Company. Run by his two sons James and Carroll, the store operated for 29 years.

BUTLER BROTHERS AT THE FLATIRON BUILDING. The Flatiron Building was not only the home to Butler's Valley Catering Company, but the large Butler family lived in the top floors. Ned and his brother Charles Butler stand in the doorway of their family home and business. Only fresh cream sent in daily from Caughey Farm in Lyonsville was used for the Butlers' ice cream, which was delivered to Sewickley and Ambridge. Goodies, including hot chocolate, hot coffee, soda from the fountain, and sandwiches, oysters, taffy, peanut brittle, homemade Saratoga, and potato chips, were available there as well. The small restaurant provided foods and ice cream for eating in, delivery, and catering services to affairs such as weddings. Black friends and family, however, were not permitted to eat in the dining room. Instead the proprietor's wife, Harriet (Hattie), would invite her guests upstairs, where the family lived, to enjoy their ice cream there.

Flatiron Building, Sewickley, Pennsylvania

FLATIRON BUILDING EXTERIOR. The uniquely triangular building patterned after a New York structure of the same name has been identified as a historic landmark by the prestigious Pittsburgh History and Landmarks Foundation. Division Street was named as it served as the boundary between two 18th-century surveys for the depreciation lands offered to Revolutionary War veterans. Today Division Street is separated by Broad Street and functions as two separate tributaries. Division Street meets Beaver Road on an acute angle, hence the unusual footprint of this plain mansard-roofed building. (Courtesy of GALS, Susan Gaca, and Carroll Logsdon.)

GENERAL BLAKEY'S BLACKSMITH SHOP, C. 1900. Among Sewickley's early African American pioneers to be in business for himself was General Blakey. His blacksmith shop once stood at 222 School Street in Edgeworth, which intersected Chestnut Street near a location that is now covered by the Edgeworth Elementary School property. General Blakey's craft was making and repairing horseshoes. (Courtesy of the Sewickley Valley Historical Society.)

H. W. BLOCKSON AND SON HAULING. Hauling and moving was an easy business for blacks to work in, as all that was needed was a horse and wagon. Horace Blockson founded his hauling business in 1907 with the horse and wagon pictured here in front of his house on Centennial Avenue. It is interesting to note that the houses behind the horse and wagon were purchased and owned by Mary Jackson, who had formerly been enslaved, in 1875.

BLOCKSON'S FIRST TRUCK. The business's first truck was also the first truck in the Sewickley Valley used for public service. Until Ellis Blockson purchased the Indiana in 1916, he had never driven a motorized vehicle. Seemingly without hesitation, however, he made an application, paid a fee, and was issued his driver's license. The truck operated primarily in the Sewickley area, but there were no state, federal, or labor regulations, so it also traveled widely in tristate counties and made a few trips to eastern Pennsylvania, New York State, Delaware, and Maryland.

BLOCKSON WORKERS AND TRUCK. The H. W. Blockson and Son Hauling business was the largest and the most constant African American employer in the history of Sewickley Valley. Records show that in 1945 it had 51 workmen on the payroll. Pictured are some of the regulars. John Barber Sr. perhaps had the greatest longevity. In time, he also operated his own hauling business.

BLOCKSON DELUXE VAN. The business eventually graduated to this deluxe moving van that was included in its fleet of about four or five various trucks. Ellis Blockson sold his business to Jimmy and Frances Powell in 1950. The Powells continued operation of the business under the Blockson name until 1971, when the business was sold.

CLEVE WITH BICYCLE. Cleveland Wallace (better known as Cleve) started his many thriving business ventures in 1919, which included repair of motorcycles and bikes, a taxi service car rental, hauling, and selling coal and sporting goods such as guns, ammunition, and fishing tackle. It is generally known that from time to time he kept a dozen big, new quality cars for his car-renting service as well as for taxis. For communicating with his drivers, Cleve Wallace was so advanced that he had private telephones all around the valley and surrounding communities for the drivers to call into the office switchboard to check their status.

OFFICE HOURS { 9 A.M. TO 2 P.M.
{ 3 P.M TO 8 P.M.
SUNDAYS BY APPOINTMENT

PHONE
SEWICKLEY
519

DR. ADDISON L. RANDOLPH
DENTIST

432 WALNUT STREET   SEWICKLEY, PA.

BLACK BUSINESS STRIP. These ancient tiny buildings on Walnut Street once housed black businesses, including barbershops, restaurants, dress shops and tailors, and Sewickley's first African American dentist office. Dr. Addison Randolph practiced in this row of shops from the dawn of the 20th century to about 1939, when they were torn down.

These four ancient stores on Walnut Street are now being torn down. They will be replaced by modern business buildings, a notable improvement to the Village district.

DIGGS' APARTMENT BUILDING. Linwood Diggs, born in 1880, came to Sewickley in 1904. Known as one of the shrewdest businessmen around, Diggs constructed and managed a four-story apartment building on Nevin Avenue. A long-standing home for its residents, the apartment building went up around 1923 and was not to be demolished until the winter of 1994–1995. Linwood Diggs was also known to work in real estate and insurance and operated a poolroom and a barbershop.

THE BRADLEY CATERERS. Assisted by her jovial husband John "Pete" Bradley, Christina Bradley began her family catering business following the end of World War II. While Christina was busy creating such delicious delectables as her signature sticky buns, her husband was in charge of all the setting up and serving. He trained many boys and men to be fine waiters. Many reminisced about how, as young people, working for the Bradley Caterers enabled them to get their class rings, graduation photographs, and school clothes as the Bradleys employed a large number of African Americans. The Bradley Caterers served large and small banquets, parties, and events for both blacks and whites for half a century. (Courtesy of the Sewickley Herald.)

JAMES (JIM) ADDISON. More than just a photographer for his vast community, church, and civic service, James (Jim) Addison was Sewickley's Man of the Year in 1994. In addition, Addison was an Aleppo Township commissioner from 1975 to the mid-1990s. A Tuskegee Airman originally from Ardmore, Addison began writing for Philadelphia newspapers and then at the Tuskegee Air Field before his love of photography came into full bloom. A deeply appreciated servant of the community, he is considered by some as the "Teenie Harris of Sewickley."

LEONARD HARRIS. Leonard Harris, real estate and insurance businessman, started his business in 1952 and has the distinction of having the longest-operating black business in the valley. Harris conducted his business from his parents' family home on Walnut Street. At one time, the house was also the site for the Village Tea Room, a small eatery operated by his father, Lewis Harris.

RUCKER HOME ESTIMATE, 1927. Elden Rucker has kept in his archives the original estimate of the cost of supplies and materials needed for the building of his home in 1927. Building one's home was not uncommon among the blacks through the 1900s. Sarah Harris and her husband, Lewis "Snookie" Harris Jr., built their home part by part—living in the basement throughout the process. She remarks that "when it was finished it was paid for." (Courtesy of William Rucker.)

CHRISTOPHER COLVIN, PLASTERER. There were two generations worth of well-established plasterers in Christopher (Chris) Colvin's plastering business. Beginning as early as 1920, Chris Colvin's business was picked up by his son Clarence Colvin. Each worked in plastering until their deaths and sometimes shared jobs with the Parrishes, another plastering family. (Courtesy of Shirley Wormsley.)

BIX CONSTRUCTION. Bix Construction gained a strong reputation for its church buildings in Philadelphia, New Jersey, and Pittsburgh. During the middle of the 20th century, brothers George, James "Wade," and John Adams were commissioned by several black families to build homes. Having purchased a lot of land above the hills of Sewickley Valley, the brothers set about fully populating Bixwood Drive, Berdine Drive, and the land between on Duff Road with ranch-style single-family dwellings. Here Garfield and Evelyn Shaw's home is in construction on Bixwood Drive. (Courtesy of Evelyn Shaw.)

TOMMY ASTON BUILDS HIS HOME. Postal workers Curtis Branch, Robert Parrish, and Tommy Aston divided evenly a 30-acre tract of land, on which each would begin building his home. Living in the basement as they built the house above them, they went to work performing part of their labor themselves. Only Tommy Aston was unable to successfully find water and eventually moved back to his family house on Centennial Avenue. (Courtesy of Susan Aston Morris.)

DOGS AND MEN. Not only for recreation and sport, men of Sewickley Valley took to the woods and the rivers to fish and hunt for food. Other popular game of the time included raccoon, squirrels, birds, and deer. Shown here are Lewis "Snookie" Harris Jr. and Henry Evans. (Courtesy of Sarah Harris.)

Four

THE VILLAGE WITHIN

THE MASONS OF ST. JOHN'S LODGE NO. 50. Among Sewickley's oldest black organizations is the St. John's Lodge No. 50. Originally a fully Caucasian lodge, its chapter was suspended for 99 years due to its insubordination toward its worshipful master, in its refusal to admit black Masons. On June 24, 1891, 26 African Americans were initiated into Masonry by authority of the Prince Hall Grand Lodge of Pennsylvania. Consequently, St. John's Lodge and all its equipment was turned over to the new Prince Hall brethren, and they were warranted under the name and number of the suspended lodge—St. John's Lodge No. 50. "One can see a certain poetic Masonic justice in this incident," noted the anniversary issue of the *Tresle Board*. Shown in this 1940s photograph are, from left to right, (first row) Raymond Dickerson, Gilbert Brannon, James Branch, Robert Quarrels, Frank Whitlock, Thurman Crump, and Thomas Gibson; (second row) William Randolph, unidentified, Walter Brannon, James Smith, Charles Butler, Lafayette "Bud" Hunter, Walter Carter, and William Dawkins. Named after Mason charter member James G. Matthews's mother, the Louisa Chapter No. 40 chapter of Easter Stars was chartered on August 17, 1921. Among its charter members are Mary L. Matthews, worthy matron; Sarah Collins, associate matron; and James G. Matthews, worthy patron.

WILSON'S CORNET BAND. The Wilson's Cornet Band is shown here on the front steps of the Broad Street School about 1906. From left to right are (first row) Samuel Gray, Charles Mossett, John Turner (the little fellow beside the big drum), Charles Anderson, Prof. Mahon C. Wilson, and John Gray (with small drum); (second row, directly behind the large drum) James Reese, Frank Gray, and Archie Turner; (third row) Horace Blockson, Edward Turner, Charles Coleman, Robert Maze, John Brown, Henry Washington, and Ellis Blockson; (fourth row) Frank Hunter, Fletcher Brown, William Patterson, Benjamin Blockson, William Kilson, Frank Wainwright, and William Fisher.

MAHON C. WILSON. Considered a professor of music, Mahon C. Wilson, founder of the Wilson's Concert Band, was affectionately called by his band members "Fess Wilson." Wilson and his band played for both whites and blacks in events including Pittsburgh parades, lawn fetes, church events, and social gatherings as well as the opening of the Sewickley Bridge in 1911. In the program shown, Fess Wilson is listed four times: first as the author, twice as performer, and last as having arranged the concert's finale, "My Jesus I Love Thee."

Programme.

1 Opening Chorus—Praise the Lord Our God
                                    . . . . Sweney
                  CHORUS.
2 Address on Music . . . . . .
                  REV. RANDOLPH.
3 Schottische—Among the Flowers . Paul Enor
                  MANDOLIN CLUB.
4 Soprano Solo—Goodbye Sweet Day . .
                  MRS. E. W. BROWN.
5 Waltz—Seaside . . . . R. L. Weaver
                  STRING QUARTETTES.
6 Female Quartette—A Song of Spring . Stone
   MRS. BROWN, MAYS. WILSON AND MISS BROWN.
7 Piano Duett—National Guards . . R. Carl
                  MRS. BROWN AND MR. P. BROWN.
8 Violin Solo—Angels Serenade . G. Braga
                  MR. J. BOWMAN.
9 March—Sewickley Enterprise Club M. C. Wilson
                  MANDOLIN CLUB.
10 Bass Solo—Hundred Fathoms Deep . Shattuck
                  MR. GEORGE HINES.
11 Guitar Solo—Fantasie Brillante . Frank Eaton
                  MAHLON C. WILSON.
12 Vocal Solo—I'm Longing For My Kentucky
                  Home . . . . Mullen
                  MR. R. L. MAYS
13 Cornet Solo—The Conqueror Polka Giovanini
                  MR. MAHLON C. WILSON.
14 Male Quartette—Watchman Tell Us . White
15 Finale—My Jesus I Love Thee
                  Gordon (arranged by M. C. Wilson)
                  ENTIRE CLUB.

Ball Team of Sevy.

EARLY BASEBALL TEAM. This is a photograph of an early black baseball team in Sewickley. This undated photograph is part of the scrapbook of Temora Haynes, who worked as a domestic in the valley for many years. She was one of Sewickley's eldest when she died at the age of 105.

HAWTHORNE CLUB. Founded by Martha W. Gibson on October 9, 1914, the Hawthorne Club originally organized to promote the welfare and progress of black women of the Sewickley Valley. The club expanded its concerns to include state and national objectives. Early members were active in the suffragette movement, worked with home front World War I efforts, and donated their handiwork to the needy. More recently, the Hawthorne Club has contributed locally to churches, the Sewickley Community Center (SCC), the Sewickley Public Library, the Care and Development Center, and WQED and holds a lifetime membership in the NAACP. For most of its existence the Hawthorne Club was a federated club member of the Pennsylvania State Federation of Negro Women's Clubs and also the National Association of Colored Women's Clubs with several of its local members serving as state officers and on national committees. Pictured above in the mid-1960s are, from left to right, (first row) Emily Snowden, Anna Hedge, Martha Naylor, Irma Kohler, Carrie Farrington, and Essie Rodgers; (second row) Alma Kohler, Grace Whitlock, Virginia Hearns, Lillian Shannon, Susan Blockson, Velma Diggs, Pearl Lee, Bettie Cole, Mildred Addison, Coretha Farmer, and Virginia Hailstock. Hosting their 83rd anniversary luncheon below are, from left to right, (first row) Leona Calloway, Velma Diggs, Hattie Cole, Virginia Hailstock, and Carolyn Jones; (second row) Emily Snowden; (third row) Pearl Lee, Daisy Crawford, and Mildred Nash; (fourth row) Jane Kohler and Sarah Dickens; (fifth row) Coretha Farmer, Bettie Cole, and Betty Addison; (sixth row) Gerri Collins.

MARY CHERRY. The Harriet Tubman Guild was organized on July 22, 1915, when 12 Christian women met at the home of Winona Idell Lincoln. The purpose of the club was to help the women's auxiliary of the Union Baptist Association (now known as the Allegheny Union Baptist Association) provide food and other household necessities for the Aged Minister's and Layman's Home. Sewickley's chapter (the Valley Chapter) of the Harriet Tubman Guild was organized by Mary Cherry in the early 1940s. Early prompting by Winona Idell Lincoln herself in her Pittsburgh high school chapter encouraged Mary Cherry to begin a local chapter when she moved here. The Valley Chapter included charter members Virginia Brannon, Dorothy Butler, Ella Capps, J. F. Dunn, Anna Harris, Mary "Mae" Johnston, Elva Knox, Frances Powell, Carrie Rainer, and Elizabeth Harp, who began their chapter with an installation tea at the SCC. Here Mary Cherry and her husband, Lawrence, pose for a portrait. (Courtesy of Grace Cherry King.)

NAACP. Sewickley Valley participated in a local chapter of the NAACP. During the 1940s, the organization fought to hire more blacks at the Sewickley Post Office. Lewis N. Harris Sr. was known for going door to door year after year in an effort to make sure that every black person in the valley was a member. He is pictured with Milt Farrington on his left. Other active members through the years include James Matthews, George Adams, Jimmy Lee, Harold Parker, Jim Addison, Mamie Smith, Alfred Smith, Thelma Wallace, Coretha Robinson, Alma Kohler, Lucille Blair, and Roberta Banks.

THE JUST US GIRLS. The Just Us Girls Club was one of the most popular social clubs in the valley, starting in the early 1940s and lasting well into the 1950s or more. These young ladies were best known for their fabulous annual fashion shows held at the Post 450 Pavilion. Proceeds were used for the benefit of the SCC. Shown here in the mid-1940s with Mary Dee, popular radio DJ, are, from left to right, (first row) Jean Mitchell, Jennie Ford, Dorothy Cottom, Mary Dee, Ruth Whaley, Elnora Turner, Hattie Cole, Blanch Lee, and Correne Branch; (second row) Bettie Cole, Pearl Turner, Margaret Colvin, Vivienne Pickett, Catherine King, Edna Jenkins, and Ruth Brooks.

GIRL RESERVES. The Girl Reserves was an affiliated YMCA national program that would later be called the Y-Teens. The organization was started in the early 1940s by Bettie Cole. Later Mary Cherry became sponsor, and during such time, the Y-Teens went on several trips and attended various Y-Teen seminars and meetings with their sister chapters. Pictured from left to right are Christine Dye, Louise Burke, Temora Brooks, Alva Shaw, Constance Calloway, and Grace Cherry.

LADIES REVUE. Velma Henderson and Isabel (Bell) Stotts are heralded as the originators of the SCC's Ladies Guild. Together they thought up the Ladies Revue, a unique fun-type feature for the great dedication program for the new gymnasium and lounge addition to the SCC in February 1960. Velma Henderson, Bell Stotts, and Alma Kohler, each on the center's board of directors at the time, were instrumental in promoting the revue. From the Ladies Revue stemmed the Ladies Guild as those "approximately 25 ladies banded together in work and purpose as they did in song and dance to organize the guild for the purpose of enhancing the center, and its new addition." (Courtesy of the Sewickley Community Center.)

DANIEL B. MATTHEWS HISTORICAL SOCIETY. The society was originally founded by Susan Blockson for the purpose of compiling and preserving records for St. Matthews African Methodist Episcopal Zion Church of Sewickley. Over the years, however, the society's endeavors have expanded to research, preserve, and promote the general study of the community as well as all black history. From left to right are (first row) Martha Naylor, Virginia Hailstock, Susan Blockson (chairman), and Hattie Cole (treasurer); (second row) James Matthews (vice chairman), Charles Butler (custodian), Walter Carter, Ellis Blockson, and Frank Whitlock.

SENIOR CITIZENS CLUB OF SEWICKLEY. This 1974 image pictures, from left to right, Virginia Hailstock, Ruth Tucker, and Rebecca Ford. Rebecca Ford, who enjoyed working with and helping senior citizens, was founder and first president of the club. For years, she and her husband, Danny, would cook, serve luncheons, and entertain the valley's seniors. Ruth Tucker, director of adult services for Allegheny County, is presenting the National Council of Senior Citizens' charter. Virginia Hailstock assisted Rebecca Ford and her Senior Club, serving as longtime president and dedicated worker. The disbanded club met at and was affiliated with the SCC. Virginia Hailstock, ardent church, community, and civic worker, retired after 23 years in the State Department of Public Welfare to become the executive director for the Lemington Home for the Aged in Pittsburgh until she retired.

SEWICKLEY HIGH SCHOOL CLASS OF 1924. History notes that African American children regularly appear alongside whites in Sewickley's vintage class photographs. While segregation was not instituted among the schoolrooms, blacks were discouraged from full participation in student life. They could not be involved in student government or join the Hi-Y Club or drama club. Restricted to sports "suitable for Blacks" and unable to go to the YMCA where school teams like golf and swimming were conducted, blacks had limited options. James Anderson and Edith O. Harris are part of Sewickley High School's graduating class in 1924. (Courtesy of the Quaker Valley School District.)

SEWICKLEY PUBLIC SCHOOL ON BROAD STREET, 1894. Sewickley Public School stood on Broad Street, taking up the full block between Broad Street and Chestnut Street and Thorn and Beaver Streets. Completed in June 1894, this school took the place of the previous one-room schoolhouses in and around Sewickley Village and marked the formal merger of townships and municipalities to form Quaker Valley. William Stockton and Julia Virginia Kirk were the first African Americans to graduate from Sewickley High School in 1892 and 1893, respectively. (Courtesy of the Quaker Valley School District.)

SEWHI 1907 FOOTBALL TEAM. In 1906, Frank Whitlock was the only black person to play football on Sewickley High School's first football team. His field performance and agility would earn him the nickname "Snake Hips" and set a standard of excellence for African Americans competing in Sewickley schools' sports. His son Kenneth Whitlock would set a personal best and unchallenged record when he kicked a 96-yard punt for Virginia State College in 1946. The Sewhi (Sewickley High School) 1907 team is pictured here, including Hays, Taggert, Cunningham, Karne, Burns, Lake, Jackson, Derr, McPherson, Allswelt, Brush, Cunningham, Tallant, Hegner, Whitlock, Kelly, and Ball. (Courtesy of Kenneth Whitlock.)

SEWHI FOOTBALL TEAM, 1933. Schoolmate Jerry Vescio identified Sewhi 1933 football team members as, from left to right, (first row) Craig Whitlock, Jimmy Krause, Meredith McCandless, Lou Malone, David Rupert, and Jack Luty; (second row) coach Bill Duncan, Philip Hahn, George Joseph, Jimmy Graham, Pete Ford, and head coach Stan Stroup; (third row) manager Charlie Wehrum, Howard Branch, Noel Fisher, Bob Lutz, Hayes Wells, Mitchell Ford, and manager Charlie Hunter; (fourth row) manager Ed Bradel and manager Ken Brown. (Courtesy of Correne Branch.)

DEDICATORY SERVICES
Colored Young Men's Christian Association.
At St. Matthew's A. M. E. Zion Church, Sunday, May 25th, 1913.

FRANK W. WHITLOCK, President.

JAMES C. LIGHTFOOT, Vice President.

THE COLORED YMCA. The Colored YMCA's formal dedication commenced on May 25, 1913, with three days of programs, services, and speakers. White dignitaries and notable blacks from Pittsburgh such as Ralph Harbison, Bayard Christy, and attorney Robert L. Vann were in attendance as other choirs and soloists shared and performed. Original board members included Frank W. Whitlock, president; James C. Lightfoot, vice president; James M. Ford, secretary; James W. Reese, assistant secretary; David S. Curtis; Arthur W. Watts; Kelley W. Miner; and W. J. Brooks. The advisory board held B. H. Christy, A. L. Mould, J. T. Peters, T. M. Kramer, S. B. Handy, J. A. Emery, and W. L Clause. John W. Budden was the first general secretary (director). Interestingly the second secretary (director), serving between 1914 and 1917, is recorded as Joseph William Bowers, the grandfather of Sewickley's first African American ophthalmologist, Dr. Richard Bowers.

THE COLORED YMCA. The Colored YMCA was the first major milestone in the black recreational and social history of Sewickley. Having its beginnings on Walnut Street, it was thus referred to as the Walnut Street YMCA. It originally was occupied as St. Matthews African Methodist Episcopal Zion Church's first building.

PUBLIC SCHOOL PAVILION, EXTERIOR. The long-demolished pavilion stood near the edge of Sewickley Public School's playground, along Chestnut Street, and was the host of much activity among the black community. Programs and organizations made good use of the playground and the space just outside the facility.

PUBLIC SCHOOL PAVILION, INTERIOR. This large, accessible facility had served the African American community as its basketball court, gymnasium, and auditorium since the formation of Colored YMCA and continued in that capacity for nearly five decades. During the 1930s through the mid-1950s, Elizabeth Harp Perry, assistant director of the SCC, conducted programs in the Sewickley Public School's pavilion and playground, most memorable being the nursery, preschool, and Sewik Summer Camp.

CARDINALS GIRLS' BASKETBALL TEAM. Louise Maze chaperoned the Cardinals, the Colored YMCA girls' basketball team, during the 1920s. Pictured here are, from left to right, (first row) Louise Maze, Dorothy Brown, Jennie Butler, Helen Matthews, Elva Brown, Marie Maze, and Louella Toliver; (second row) assistant coach Richard Brown, Florence Ford, Vivian Ford, Laura "Snookie" Butler, Mildred Maze, Edith Whitlock, and coach "Sing" Grey. Unfortunately, no known photograph was found for the Colored YMCA's men's magnificent and legendary team of that era, the Thundering Herd.

SCC BASKETBALL TEAM, 1952. This photograph pictures the winning United Neighborhood House League champions, senior division, in 1952. Playing for the team are, from left to right, (first row) unidentified, Victor Green, Ronald "Chun" Tucker, and Lou Bonkins; (second row) Ritzy Lee, Donald Shakleford, Girard Williams, Edward Lewis, David Jackson, Victor Jones, Alonzo Gilmore, and Charles "Skip" Redwing. Edward Lewis was the center director at that time. (Harris Studios photograph, courtesy of the Sewickley Community Center.)

SCC BASKETBALL TEAM. A later community center basketball team photograph shows, from left to right, (first row) Kenny Stotts, Johnny Harrison, Felton Martin, Alvin Jones, and Billy Joe Leverett; (second row) Harry Buntin, William Turner, Theodore (Teddy) White, William Teamor, and Fred Council. (Charles Green photograph, courtesy of the Sewickley Community Center.)

Y-FIELD, CHADWICK STREET. An open field, which originally housed the Gibbs family's huge vegetable garden, became an African American hot spot early in the 20th century. Known by blacks as the Y-Field, because of the Colored YMCA's activity there, it officially came under black ownership when Mrs. A. Wilson Campbell donated it to the Colored Sewickley Community Center in 1944. Later when the American Legion Post 450 moved onto Chadwick Street, across from the field, the two organizations would often sponsor events together and enthusiastically support each other.

THE WALNUT STREET Y BASEBALL TEAM, MAY 1912. An early snapshot of this baseball team underlines the enthusiasm for what is known as an "all-American sport." Seated here in front of their building on Walnut Street is the Cubs. This photograph dated Saturday, May 4, 1912, pictures, from left to right, Spencer Brown (mascot, seated on the ground); (first row) John Waters (fielder), William Curtis (first base), Christopher Richardson (fielder), James Reese (manager), Clarence Reese (right field), and Cecil Campbell (fielder); (second row) George Ward (first base), Elijah Brown (catcher), Frank Hailstock (pitcher), Charles Kirk (pitcher), and James Reynolds (third base). Standing to the right is coach Alphonso Burnard.

SEWICKLEY COLORED COMMUNITY CENTER. When the Walnut Street YMCA became damaged by flood, its inability to secure permanent space would lead to its gradual decline. The Sewickley Valley Ministerial Association under the leadership of Rev. Louis Hirshson and the Young Men's Club (a group of progressive African American young men) along with a group of prominent local citizens joined together to establish the Sewickley Colored Community Center. Temporarily housed at Triumph Baptist Church, the new center first opened its doors on February 5, 1937, to register a total of 40 girls and boys for handcrafts, social clubs, and sports each day from 3:30 p.m. to 8:30 p.m. Over 20 years later, the organization legally dropped the word *colored* from its name and was then known as the Sewickley Community Center (SCC). Officially, the SCC's first home was on Division Street, where the center operated from 1939 to 1951. Adjacent to its building (the former William Blakey house) on Division Street was the SCC's recreation/social building. Larger gatherings, banquets, and fairs would have been held here.

SCC ADULT SEWING CLASS. Held at the SCC on Division Street was this adult sewing class. Class participants are, from left to right, Elizabeth Harp, Bell Stotts, Margaret Turner, Christine Bradley, unidentified, Annie Hedge, Sarah Johnson, Mabel Lightfoot, Ruby Campbell, and Anna Harris. The instructor, Mabel Lightfoot (standing, center), was an accomplished seamstress in the valley, sewing for the wealthy white ladies. Among other notable and successful African American seamstresses were Ida Wilson and Harriet Hailstock.

SCC BRIDGE CLASS. This bridge class in 1947 instructed by Theodore "Teets" Taylor (standing) includes playing students Daisy Thomas, Laura Wilson, Pearl Lee, Mittie Bruson, Bea Blake, Yvonne Knox, Ruby Woodley, Addie Hayes, Vivian Stewart, Margaret Colvin, and Bell Stotts.

SCC MOTHER'S CLUB SPONSORS NURSERY SCHOOL. The Mother's Club was from the Tots and Parents Pre-School on Division Street in 1947. Identified participants are children (from left to right) Bonnie Withrow, Janet Lee, Penny Branch, Frank "Hank" Hailstock, John Tyler, Diane Ackles, Butch Cole, Betty Mitchell, Kenny Stotts, ? Austin, James "Spike" Lee, and Sam Turner. Mothers are, from left to right, Beatrice Austin, Helen Withrow, Pearl Lee, Elnora Turner, Amelia Tyler, Hattie Cole, Correne Branch, Jean Mitchell, Bell Stotts, Blanche Lee, and Alma Ackles.

SCC GIRL SCOUT TROOP. This intermediate Girl Scout troop in 1947 is meeting at the Division Street location. Pictured from left to right are (first row) Julia "Sissy" Cottom, Vera Smith, Jane Pierce, Agnes Dye, Louise Jackson, and Mamie Smith; (second row) Louise Burke, Yvonne Williams, Elizabeth Harp Percy, Dolly Williams, Grace Cherry, and Connie Calloway. (Ted Moss photograph, courtesy of the Sewickley Community Center.)

ATHLETIC BANQUET, 1947. The Sewickley Colored Community Center would take every opportunity to reward its achievers. Shown here is an athletic banquet in 1947 taking place at the community center's recreation building on Division Street.

THE SCC, CHADWICK STREET. The center grew and, needing more space, moved to its present location on 15 Chadwick Street, which was donated by Margaret Campbell in 1951. Huge strides and flourishing programs were implemented in this space. Within the decades, the Sewickley Colored Community Center would become the SCC when the reference to race was legally removed from its title.

THE COMMUNITY CENTER SERVICE CLUB. The Women's Service Club was an integral part of the SCC. In fact, it has been said that it "came with" the center. When Jim Anderson took leadership in 1948, he invited a group to support and raise money for the efforts of the center, which was the start of the service club. Here the service club is shown presenting the center with two important gifts. The one shown above is the first PA system given to the center. And the second is its first station wagon. With its move, the center now had a need to offer transportation for its members (especially those with nursery school children) traveling from within the village to its farther location on Chadwick Street. Throughout the years, the community center service club's annual trips were its main fund-raiser, which also provided a great source of fun and entertainment for all who participated.

BROWNIES AND GIRL SCOUTS, 1955. Brownies and Girls Scouts pose for their shot developed by Harris Studios in Pittsburgh. Shown here are, from left to right, (first row) Pansy Turner, Connie Smith, Gwen Smith, Joyce Blair, Rita Benson, and ? Witherow; (second row) Annette "Bunny" Brunson, Isabelle "Blondee" Martin, Anita Thomas, Joyce Cherry, Beverly Lee, and Mildred Massie; (third row) Betty Mitchell, Angela Rush, unidentified, Jackie Cotton, Charlotte Brannon (in back), Janice Warren (in front), Diane Ackles, Janet Lee, Barbara Brannon, and Earlene Massie. (Harris Studios photograph; courtesy of the Sewickley Community Center.)

SCC BOY SCOUTS AND COMMITTEE, 1955. Boy Scouts pose for their group photograph at the SCC on Chadwick Street. Included in this photograph are, from left to right, (first row) James "Spike" Lee, Hank Hailstock, Marion Wallace, Allen Crawford, Kenny Stotts, and Dickie Lee; (second row) Thad Cook Jr., Chuckie Turner, Clarence Craft, Tommy Brannon, Butch Cole, and James "Choo" Wormsley; (third row) unidentified, Charlie Turner, Rowland Crawford, Dick Lee, Thaddeus Cook, Jesse Stotts, James "Seymour" Wormsley, Rosenwald Witherow, and Thomas Brannon. (Harris Studios photograph; courtesy of the Sewickley Community Center.)

SCC, c. 1960. In later years, the SCC would complete renovations, adding and expanding meeting rooms and building a new tennis court. Edgar (Ed) Gray Sr. was instrumental in attaining the tennis court, which was completed in 1952. Center custodian for about 50 years, Gray was a tennis enthusiast all his life.

SCC, c. 1972. The outdoor swimming pool with adjacent kiddie pool was conceived in 1968 while Stanley Rideout was the SCC's director. The pool came to fruition in July 1971 and was named the Rae Community Pool because of a substantial contribution from the prominent Henry Rae family. With the added space and Post 450 as the SCC's neighbor beginning in 1951, the northwest end of Chadwick Street became a beacon of entertainment and recreation that filled a spectrum of interests and activity.

FALL FESTIVAL AT POST 450. The community center Y-Teens and the Just Us Girls (a popular social club) man their booths at the annual fall festival held at the Post 450 Pavilion. The Walter Robinson American Legion Post 450 became an attractive optional location for community events once the post moved to the old Sewickley train station (across from the SCC's new Chadwick Street location) and added a pavilion. Shown spanning both booths are, from left to right, Catherine King Killins, Hattie Cole, Ruth Whaley, Joanne Hicks-Cook, Leona Fisher-Hubbard, Christine Dye, Laura Cooper, and Geraldine Cottom Law.

RECOGNITION BANQUET. The pavilion of the Walter Robinson American Legion Post 450 (constructed in the mid-1940s) was a welcome addition to the valley's African American community as a facility to hold many social and cultural events. This recognition banquet for the community center clubs was sponsored by the center in May 1948 and held in the Post 450 Pavilion. Standing is guest speaker Mal Good of Pittsburgh, who later became the first African American news anchorman on a major television network. Seated alongside him from left to right are Jim R. C. Lee, Heywood Patterson, Edward Lewis (the center director), and Ike Kohler. Recognized at the far end are Frank and Grace Whitlock, Pearl Lee, Dorothy Blair, Helen Gould, and Addie Hayes.

POST 450 ANNUAL MARCH OF DIMES BALL. Hostesses for the annual March of Dimes Ball around 1955 are, from left to right, (first row) Alma Kohler, Georgia Gould, Minnie Browning, Bettie Cole, Fleda Blake, Catherine King, and Edna Jenkins; (second row) Jean Mitchell, Vera Rucker, Ruth Brooks, Ruth Whaley, Hattie Cole, Ann Boswell, Etta Cook, Elnora Turner.

PROM PHOTOGRAPH. At the Post 450 Pavilion around the late 1940s–1950s, the African American youth of Sewickley Valley gather for an exclusive prom. Discouraged from participating in otherwise public events, the community often relied on itself for socializing.

78

Five

SERVICEMEN AND
THEIR POST

HAULING CANNONS UP BROAD STREET TO SEWICKLEY CEMETERY, APRIL 1905. African Americans of the Sewickley Valley have participated in wartime battles both on the field and the home front throughout their long history. They were wounded, and many were psychologically scarred by the devastation of varied battles and human destruction. And some died. This photograph illustrates the community's air of nationalism at the dawn of the 20th century and community participation in military affairs. Two 15-inch Rodman cannons made for the independence of Boston Harbor by the Fort Pitt Foundry were hauled up Broad Street to the Sewickley Cemetery, where they would remain until collected for the scrap drive in 1943. Weighing 15,000 pounds each, they would contribute several tons of iron to the wartime effort. (Courtesy of the Sewickley Valley Historical Society.)

MEN LEAVING FOR WORLD WAR I. Shown here at the intersection of Broad and Beaver Streets on October 27, 1917, are men leaving for World War I. Identified kneeling are ladies of the Red Cross: Martha B. Madison, Laura Ford-Wilson, Mary Johnson, Miss Parrish, Martha Gibson, Blanche Parker, Virginia Hailstock, Mary Catherine Kirk-Delaney, Alice Tucker, Edna Crawford, Dorothy Madison, Vertle Brown-Green, Flora Madison, Virginia Tyman, Eliza Cornish-Mitchell, Marietta Townsend-Jones, Marie Peterson, and Marietta Smith. Standing with a flower in their lapel (to indicate those leaving for war) are Leo Campbell, David Waters,

Marshall Taylor, Leroy Williams, George Ward, Clarence Reese, Archie Townsend, Lawrence Berry, David Cole, Napoleon Collins, Howard Brown, Vernon Lovett, Tally Ralph Parrish, Ellis A. Blockson, James Reynolds, Henry Parrish, and David S. Curtis. Among those in the background are Professor Brown, Elmer Parker, Edward Brooks, James Carrington, Elizabeth Smith, Clyde Jones, Frank Pollard, Beverly Gilkerson, James Smith, Rev. A. W. Watts, chief of police Beatly, Rev. O. J. Remson, a Mr. Jamison, Everette Gorham, Temora Haynes, Mary Madision, and William Dudley.

First Aid Class of Sewickley

First World War

First Trained Afro-American Red Cross

Standing (left to right)—Mrs Ellie Blakey, Miss Laura Ford, Mrs Lillian Monroe, Mrs Mattie Delk, Miss Lena Dickerson, Mrs Martha Gibson.

Sitting—Miss Mary Kirk, Miss Mary Johnson, Mrs Grace Whitlock, Mrs Lawrence Madison, Miss Lillian Abner, Mrs Mary Arnold, Miss Bessie Kirk.

A tinge of war preparation was given at an entertainment at St Matthews' African Methodist Episcopal Zion Church in Sewickley, Thursday evening, when a group of Red Cross aids gave an exhibition under the direction of Dr E E Bach, the sociological director of Ellsworth Collieries Company. This class has taken the required examination after weeks of instructions with Dr Bach and Dr Charles Murray of this city, and

"First-Aid" Workers in America

gave demonstrations Thursday even in rolling bandages, finger, hand, and knee; four-tail bandages, jaw, and head; a stretcher drill, and an artificial respiration from drowning.

"This class has the honor of being only colored first-aid Red Cross class America," said Dr Bach, "and we proud of them." There are also th other members, Miss Myrtle Brown, Mary Langan and Miss Kate Ford. was through the unstinted efforts of Alexander Laughlin of Sewickley this class was made possible, and co-operation of Mrs Ralph Harbison, S C Scott and Mrs C M South. president of the first-aid group is Lawrence Madison, who is an arc worker, and is enthusiastically doing bit for world democracy.

AFRICAN AMERICAN RED CROSS CLASS OF SEWICKLEY. In case needed on the homeland, these ladies were trained in a variety of emergency procedures during World War I. As quoted in the newspaper clipping above, "'This class has the honor of being the only colored first-aid Red Cross class in America,' said Dr. Bach, 'and we are proud of them.'"

Within the photograph:

1917 — In France
506th ENGINEERS BAND
Three charter members of Post 450 Seated, second from Left:
Ellis A. Blockson (Clarinet) Seated, second above, right of
drum; Howard E. Brown (Trombone) Tall man, standing, behind H.
Brown; Tally Ralph Parrish (Baritone horn)

506TH ENGINEERS BAND. Three members of the all–African American 506th Engineers Band pictured here in France in 1917 during World War I are from Sewickley and, in fact, are three charter members of Post 450. Seated second from the left is Ellis Blockson on the clarinet, second above and to the right of the drum is Howard Brown on the trombone, and the tall man standing behind him on the bass horn is Tally Ralph Parrish.

WALTER RALEIGH ROBINSON. Walter Raleigh Robinson, private in Company K-803, Pioneer Infantry died on January 23, 1921. As Sewickley's first black veteran to die as a result of wartime injury, Post 450 was named for him. The Walter Robinson American Legion Post 450 is the lasting memorial for the African American men who fought and served in America's battles. The legion was founded on September 28, 1922, by ex-servicemen of Sewickley Valley Col. Robert Way and senior vice commander of Sewickley Post No. 4 and comrade Harry Winston of Coraopolis. (Courtesy of the Sewickley Valley Historical Society.)

OLD SEWICKLEY TRAIN STATION. The legionnaires first met from house to house until they got the vacant building of the disbanded St. John's African Methodist Episcopal Zion Church on Elizabeth Street during the 1930s. Following that, they met upstairs in the Park Building on Beaver Street where they secured a liquor license. That building, however, was condemned during World War II, and they were forced to move. Meanwhile, the former Sewickley train station, built in 1887, was unknowingly awaiting its new command. (Courtesy of the Sewickley Valley Historical Society.)

MOVING THE "OLD STATION" TO CHADWICK ST.

LOADING THE OLD TRAIN STATION, OCTOBER 1929. The old Sewickley train station was loaded onto flatcars via a specially built track that reached from the station to the flatcar tops. Then by winch and tractor, the building was pulled for 20 minutes on iron rollers onto the flatcars and transported by steam engine to Chadwick Street. The feat was so incredible that it made *Ripley's Believe It or Not*, a syndicated newspaper cartoon in 1962. (Courtesy of the Sewickley Valley Historical Society.)

MOVING THE OLD TRAIN STATION. With appreciation for the architectural value, it was determined to move Sewickley's old train station rather than to demolish it upon the relocation of the railroad tracks. As motor vehicle transportation became increasingly popular, provisions for the road, Ohio River Boulevard or Route 65, were made, and the railroad was moved closer to the river. (Courtesy of the Sewickley Valley Historical Society.)

POST 450. While Sewickley's new train station was built on Chadwick Street, on the southeast side of the Sewickley Bridge, on its opposite end, the old Sewickley train station made its new home. At first it was occupied as a family dwelling during the 1930s and 1940s, reserving a place for the Union Aid Society to store donated items. However, the Walter Robinson American Legion Post 450 would purchase Sewickley's old train station on December 30, 1944.

VETERANS OF WORLD WAR II. Included in the World War II veterans are Otho Stewart, Thomas (Tommy) Aston, Wilbert Warner, Lucious Hugley, James R. C. (Jim) Lee, John Curtis, David Ingram, and Lavelle Colvin.

86

LADIES' AUXILIARY. The ladies' auxiliary was organized in December 1926 and chartered the following April. All married to veterans, the list of charter members includes Susan Blockson, Lucy Blockson, Rachel Brown, Mary Crawford, Ada Ferguson, Lula Grooms, Lucille Higginbotham, Emma T. Moore, Elizabeth Parrish, Mary L. Taylor, Daisy Tinsley, and Louise Williams. The ladies' auxiliary was known to conduct a variety of fund-raisers and offer its services at the Sewickley Valley Hospital. However, most familiar may be its annual tea. Shown during the 1960s are, from left to right, (first row) Harriet Hailstock, Juanita Thomas, Jennie Ford, Dorothy Blair, and Temora Haynes; (second row) Vera Rucker, Cora Lee Steele, Bessie Douglas, Susan Blockson, Isabelle Smith, and Lucille Blair.

LADIES' AUXILIARY ANNIVERSARY TEA. Hosted at the Walter Robinson American Legion Post 450, the ladies' auxiliary holds its annual tea. Shown here are, from left to right, Anita Thomas (little girl in front); (first row) Susan Blockson, Annie Hedge, Sarah Ogletree, Georgia Gould, Etta Cook, Bettie Cole, and Hattie Clay; (second row) Marion Henley, Temora Haynes, Barbara L. Ford Carpenter, Lucille Gore, Juanita Thomas, Jennie Ford, Marion Lee, Pearl Lee, Bell Stotts, Hattie Cole, Lucille Blair, Cora Lee Steele Ross, Mittie "Hattie" Gordon, and Aleane Brown; (third row) Vivienne Stewart and Ruth Whaley.

The Sewickley Tuskegee Airmen

Lt. Robert Higginbotham

Sgt. Frank Hailstock, Jr.*

Sgt. James Addison*

Lt. William Johnston, Jr.

Lt. William Curtis*

Lt. William Gilliam*

Lt. Curtis Branch*

Lt. Mitchell Higginbotham

*deceased

TUSKEGEE AIRMEN OF SEWICKLEY VALLEY. Eight African American men from Sewickley Valley have been identified as Tuskegee Airmen. As was noted during a 2005 celebration in Sewickley, eight airmen—Mitchell and Robert Higginbotham, William Johnston Jr., Jim Addison, Curtis Branch, William Curtis Jr., William Gilliam, and Frank Hailstock Jr.—all hailed from a three-mile area stretching across Sewickley Valley from Leetsdale, through Sewickley Village to Allepo Township. (Courtesy of the Daniel B. Matthews Historical Society.)

Regis Bobonis Sr. Regis Bobonis Sr., a newer member of the Sewickley community and a veteran himself, has actively pursued research of the Tuskegee Airmen of the valley. To date, he and others of the Daniel B. Matthews Historical Society have identified some eight Tuskegee Airmen, helping to gain national recognition for their service and achievements in a celebratory event held by the Daniel B. Matthews Historical Society. (Courtesy of Leslie Bobonis Myers.)

In Tribute to Our Billy

In June 1945, as his proud parents look on, William Johnston, Jr. of Sewickley was pinned with his 2nd Lt. Bars by his sister, Martha (now Mrs. Martha Johnston Wilkins of Oberlin, Ohio).

William Johnston Jr. *Our Sweetwater: A Journal of African American History, Sewickley, PA* and a program flyer from the Daniel B. Matthews Historical Society's tribute to Sewickley's Tuskegee story included this sponsoring tribute. (Courtesy of the Daniel B. Matthews Historical Society.)

WILLIAM RUCKER. Sewickley native William Rucker sits in his jeep as part of the 5th Army Transportation Corps during World War II. (Courtesy of William Rucker.)

CLARENCE E. COLVIN. Clarence E. Colvin, in uniform, served in World War II and is listed in the Sewickley Valley honor roll dedication ceremony. (Courtesy of Shirley Wormsley.)

FOUR SONS OF FLORENCE DIGGS. Florence Diggs made headline news when it was discovered that her four sons had all been called into military service during World War II. The news article pictures, from left to right, Sgt. Stanley Diggs, Cpl. Henry Diggs, Florence Diggs, Pvt. Lucien Diggs, and Pvt. John Diggs. At that time, all were still serving within the states. Florence Diggs was the widow of Linwood Diggs, of Diggs' Apartment Building.

THREE GENERATIONS OF SERVICEMEN. These men, all of the same family, served in four separate conflicts: World War I, World War II, the Korean Conflict, and the Vietnam War. Standing from left to right are Matthew King, Harvey King, James "Choo" Wormsley, and Harvey "Butch" King Jr. (Courtesy of Mattie King Butler.)

FRANK HAILSTOCK SR. Past commander of Walter Robinson American Legion Post 450 Frank Hailstock stands proud at Sewickley's bicentennial celebration. (Courtesy of the Sewickley Herald.)

MATT WORMSLEY. Unlike the conflicts of the past that spawned strong nationalistic sentiment, the Vietnam War was a long and unpopular war. Spanning from the 1950s to the 1970s, the United States' role in the war became one of the most debated issues in the nation's history. Although sometimes reluctant to talk about their participation, many blacks of the Sewickley Valley served the country as they were called. (Courtesy of Mattie King Butler.)

OUTSIDE POST 450. This was a popular gathering place outside the Walter Robinson American Legion Post 450 home during the 1940s. Friends and family gather round to watch a ball game going on at the Y-Field across the road.

INSIDE POST 450. A pavilion added to the back of the legion would give it a new and great space. Initially drawing boxing tournaments, the new pavilion would usher in Post 450's big band era from the late 1940s through the 1960s, when the post hosted such big-name bands and performers as Dizzy Gillespie, Cab Calloway, Buddy and Ella Johnson, Ruth Brown, Duke Ellington, Ella Fitzgerald, Gene Amons, Bill Doggett, "Bull Moose" Jackson, Woody Herman, Count Basie, Dinah Washington, Louis Jordan, Stan Getz, and Jackie Wilson. Shown here is Ahmad Jamal performing at Post 450.

MEMORIAL DAY PARADE. Veterans of Post 450 participate fully in Memorial Day activities. Here local World War II veterans march in the Memorial Day parade through Sewickley. Below, a Memorial Day service is held at Antioch Freewill Baptist Church.

POST 450 DRILL TEAM. Jesse Stotts formed the Walter Robinson American Legion Post 450 drill team when he noticed how much black soldiers actually enjoyed and excelled in marching. Having recently returned from service in World War II, drill team members were used to running, marching, and drilling. Their marching was strictly legitimate military precision marching with snappy, innovative movements that gave them a singular flare and excitement that was unique. Larry Jenkins, who had been an officer in the army, became the first drillmaster, with Walter Carter as the assistant. A second generation of the Post 450 drill team sprang up during the 1960s, shown below. With an appreciation for rhythm, precision, and unity, this new team recaptured the attention of the village and gave further attention to the service of the veterans of Walter Robinson American Legion Post 450. (Below, courtesy of Sarah Harris.)

This will mark the kick-off for the emerging exhibit on the history of the station building and the American Legion Post 450 and their intertwining roles in our community. Also, we are commemorating 50 years of the American Legion Social Hall (1945 - 1995). We are committed to preserving this important local landmark.

FRIENDS OF SEWICKLEY TRAIN STATION. Approaching its 100th birthday, the old Sewickley train station and Post 450's home became increasingly in need of repair and renovation. Toward that end, a group of community preservationists emerged during the 1980s. Their mission was threefold: to protect a historic building that has played a crucial role in the development of the Sewickley Valley, to provide a broad-based multiracial model for preserving a major piece of local African American heritage, and to act as a supervisory body to ensure its proper maintenance. Friends of the Old Sewickley Train Station was formed. The board of directors included Walter J. Brannon, Kenneth Whitlock, Bettie Cole, Many Applegate, Regis Bobonis Sr., William Boyd Jr., Robert Graham, Samuel Green, Grace Greene, Douglas Jackson, Cordella Jacobs, Douglas Lauffer, Eliza Nevin, Kathleen Pearson, Karen Petley, Stanley Rideout, and Richard Smith. The group determined to create a photograph exhibit highlighting the importance of Post 450 in relation to its location at the old train station and Sewickley's African American community.

POST 450 PHOTOGRAPHY EXHIBIT. A photography exhibit documenting the African American history in the Sewickley Valley was created and put on display at the post. The exhibit now hangs in the basement of St. Matthews African Methodist Episcopal Zion Church, with the Daniel B. Matthews Historical Society acting as custodians.

HISTORIC LANDMARK, 1994. As a result of the work to restore and preserve Sewickley's old train station and Walter Robinson American Legion Post 450, the building was designated as a historic landmark by the Pittsburgh History and Landmarks Foundation as the oldest nonreligious public building in Sewickley. It also stands as an irreplaceable 1887 landmark representing the magnificent era of the train. Kenneth Whitlock, Louis Lockhart, Walter Brannon, Kathleen Pearson, Eliza Cavalier, and Harry Rideout are shown in this picture from left to right.

POST 450, RESTORED. Grants and donations and fund-raising in the form of jazz concerts and a "Great Station to Station Picnic" afforded the home of Walter Robinson American Legion Post 450 a huge renovation, including restoration of the large porch area and restoration of the original facade to its bright yellow and red, which gained it the characterization of "tomato omelet." Restoration was complete in 1994.

Six

TO NAME A FEW

THE SEWICKLEY VALLEY

LAUNCHED.

THE FRANCIS J. TORRANCE NOW IN THE WATERS OF THE OHIO.

Sewickley Valley people are much interested in the launching of the new excursion boat, "Francis J. Torrance," which occurred last Saturday at Marietta, since it is to be a source of much pleasure to them next summer in its trips up and down the Ohio. There were several thousand people, many going from Pittsburg and surrounding towns, gathered to witness the event. At the proper time Captain J. M. Boyd, General Manager of the Manongahela and Ohio River Transportation Company, to which the boat belongs, stepped to the bow of the vessel and in a brief address thanked the people for their presence and detailed the purposes of the launching of the boat. He was greeted with many cheers. At the close of the speech he introduced his sister, Miss Anna Boyd, who went gracefully through the usual form of christening, saying "I christen thee Francis J. Torrance; and to thee, proud waters of the ever-beautiful Ohio, into thy arms, do I entrust her, and on thy vast bosom may ever float this stately ship."

Workmen then knocked the props from under the large structure until there remained but two, and then in a loud voice rang out the commands, "One," "Two," "Three," and the boat slowly tilted on its site and started on its ride down the ways. It brought to mind those beautiful lines:

" She starts, she moves, she seems to feel
The thrill of life along her keel."

Cheer after cheer went up, and those who took the ride hastened to Captain Boyd and congratulated him on the successful launch, and wished that the future of the boat might ever be as successful as was her beginning.

It was greatly regretted that Mr. Torrence was not able to be present otherwise the time was one long to be remembered for the pleasure.

A REWARD.

A generous reward will be given for the return to the SEWICKLEY VALLEY office of a small, brown dog, with long hair, lost on Friday evening of last week. He had no collar. Answers to the name of Ruffles.

MISS MATILDA JONSON.

The subject of our half-tone engraving, Miss Matitda Jonson, is s prodigy in the musical line. To quote a well-known professor of music: "She plays the real old negro music of fifty years ago. Rag time, as she plays it, is in its purity unadulterated with American ideas." Some time ago she purchased one of the finest autoharps on which she has no equal in her own style of playing. It is very much of a treat to hear her performance on the autoharp. She plays nearly all the stringed instruments and plays them in the real old negro style that never fails to delight the hearer. Miss Jonson is now over sixty years of age and is well known throughout the Valley, having been a servant at times in most of the old families of Sewickley.

MATILDA JONSON. According to this early newspaper clipping, Matilda Jonson was a talented student of music and engaging performer. She is noted to have served as a domestic "in most of the old families of Sewickley." She is among the first documented to serve the public with her endearing tunes.

EARLY AFRICAN AMERICAN SEWICKLEY MAIL CARRIERS AND FIREMEN. Early postmen of the Sewickley Post Office include William Blakey, James Matthews, Jim Reese, and Frank Whitlock Sr. Joseph M. Carrington served as fireman-laborer and Arthur Watts as a janitor. Among the carriers, William Blakey holds the rank as earliest appointed African American mail carrier in 1919. The 1911 photograph below taken of the Edgeworth volunteer firemen shows Sol Toliver, the first black man to serve as a fireman.

MILT FARRINGTON. Constable James "Milt" Farrington was the valley's first law enforcement officer working under the legendary justice of the peace Maggie Morgan from 1929 until his death in February 1945.

WALTER J. BRANNON. Walter J. Brannon was the first African American to serve on the Sewickley Police Department and the only African American to serve as its chief of police. Hired in 1952, he served as an officer first, then as chief beginning in 1976 until his retirement in 1992. Harold Pickett, an African American, was Sewickley Valley's second senior sergeant, beginning his service on the Sewickley police force in 1972. Harold Parker and Hardin Smith worked as special and part-time police officers for several years beginning in 1972.

101

MAKE QUAKER VALLEY FIRST IN EDUCATIO

Maintain Our Excellent Education System With Sound Financial Responsi

NOMINATE

M.M. Zahorchak	David Starr Jr.	Herbert H. Myers
(Dem.)	(Dem.)	(Rep.)
Region I	Region 2	Region 3
Dem. Pull Lever 33A	Dem. Pull Lever 33A	Rep. Pull Lever 34E
Rep. Write Name In	Rep. Write Name In	Dem. Write Name In

Non-Partisan Support Of These Candidates Will

*Assure effective communication between the Quaker Valley Board and the taxpayers.

**Assure responsible Board members to keep our education expenses in line.

*Assure proper leadership to guide the growth of our schools to meet education and population trends.

This Advertisement Paid For By:
Concerned Taxpayers Of Quaker Valley School District Committee
William Feduska, Secretary
John S. Ewing

5/12/71

SEWICKLEY HERALD   (Paid Political Announcement)

DAVID E. STARR. The first black man to serve on the Sewickley Council was David E. Starr. In addition, he was the second black on the Quaker Valley School Board, the first being Alfred D. Smith, who at that time was the director of the SCC. Starr served on the Quaker Valley School Board from 1966 to 1973 and on Sewickley Council from 1993 to 1997. Stanley Rideout was the second black on the Sewickley Council, serving four years.

PRYOR WAY. John Pryor has the distinction of being the only black man to have a street in Sewickley named after him—where he and his wife lived in a one-story cottage. Pryor was a sexton at the Presbyterian church where he "worshipped with the white folk" and assisted the church's treasurer with the collection of pew rents. Once the First National Bank opened in November 1890, Pryor was given the job of messenger, which he held until his death.

SAM HART. Sam Hart delivered newspapers most of his life up until he died, and folks in Sewickley Valley affectionately called him "the world's oldest paper boy." First selling papers independently, he worked for Sewickley News for many years. Sewickley News also provided employment for many young news carriers, including Blaine and Mark Frank, Richard Tucker, Doug Jackson, Lance Whitlock, Stevie Cottom, Sean Murphy, Carla Robinson, Dawn Patillo, and Tracey Patillo. Their first African American clerk was Ruth Gilmore.

| QV Junior High: 1955 | Nurse: 1961 | Vatican II Nun: 1967 | Principal: 1989 |

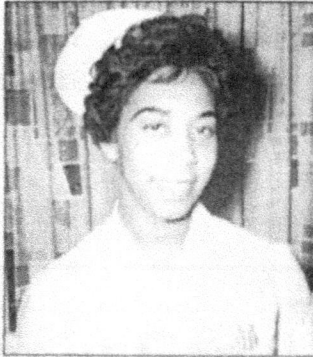

Dr. Patricia Grey: Woman of the '80

Nurse, nun, educator: Sewickley native has grown with vision for 'people of color'

By Eve Moore

"...If I have to, I can do anything. I am strong. I am invincible. I am woman..."

More than a decade ago these lyrics sung by Helen Reddy echoed the voice of a female burgeoning into a new self-assured role.

Like the dessert after a rain, this "Woman" has flourished into a force to be reckoned with. Today she can do it all.

Dr. Patricia Grey is an '80s lady.

From nurse, to nun, to educator, Dr. Grey sees her purpose as a trail-blazer — first and foremost.

A Sewickley native, the daughter of Mary and Edgar Grey who still reside on Ferry Street, Patricia's heritage begat leadership. Her maternal grand-

a shy child with a bent on altruism.

"I wanted to serve," she explains. But her mind wanted for more. She yearned to know the people she was to serve. "I wanted to know what made people tick." Teaching seemed to be the road to take.

However, according to Dr. Grey, there were kinks in the system.

"The school system did not invite me, as a black woman, to go into teaching," she says, explaining what she believed the situation was in the QV of the 1950s, not with bitterness, but with candor.

"At that time, black students were channeled into commercial rather than academic courses. This made me quite a determined woman."

Now, coupled with a longing to serve, her determination gave her a clearer focus of her future. Patricia says she sought the nursing field because it would

PATRICIA GREY. With a heart dedicated to service and the ambition to find her personal best, Patricia Grey gained local attention when by 1989, some 30 years after graduating from Sewickley High School, she had experienced an array of warm-spirited careers.

104

VELMA JACKSON. African American native Velma Jackson was the first attorney to establish her professional career in the heart of Sewickley Valley. Active in local organizations, including the Hawthorne Club, Jackson worked first in her Pittsburgh office in Gateway Center before moving her offices to the plaza on the cusp of Osborne's Ohio River Boulevard. In addition, she has been Sewickley's civil service commissioner since the early 1980s. Sewickley native Billy Martin, Esq., would gain national attention on the legal team of Monica Lewinsky during Kenneth Starr's investigation of Pres. Bill Clinton.

BLACKS AND THE SEWICKLEY VALLEY HOSPITAL. In 1923, Floyd Blair Sr. was the first African American hired at the Sewickley Valley Hospital. He worked in the laundry. Within a relatively short amount of time, huge strides have occurred with the African American community of Sewickley Valley Hospital. The first African American lab technician was James Cook. Dr. Robert Higginbotham became the first African American intern at Sewickley Valley Hospital. Dr. Edward James became the first doctor on the medical staff at Sewickley Valley Hospital in 1970. Dr. Olu Sangodeyi, a surgeon, began working in 1980 and served as president of the medical staff from 1996 to 1998. Dr. Gregory B. Patrick would become the first African American department head as the director of the pulmonary department in July 1981. The Sewickley Valley welcomed Dr. Richard Bowers, the first African American ophthalmologist, when he came in October 1991 to practice at Sewickley Valley Hospital and at the Sewickley Eye Center. The eye center now owns the building on Broad Street between Thorn and Beaver Streets and operates from the top floor there.

SHIRLEY WORMSLEY. While Frank Hailstock Jr. was the first African American male teacher within the Quaker Valley schools and Geraldine Shackleford was the first female, it was Shirley Wormsley who had the longest tenure of any African American teacher in the Quaker Valley School District. A graduate of Sewickley High School, class of 1964, Shirley Wormsley taught from 1970 until her retirement in 2003, of which 26 years were spent in the Quaker Valley School District.

QUAKER VALLEY MIDDLE SCHOOL. What was once the Sewickley High School is now the Quaker Valley Middle School, as 11 municipalities combined to form the Quaker Valley School District. Dr. Melvin Steals became the Quaker Valley School District's first African American school administrator, serving as acting principal of Osborne Elementary School first, then as assistant principal of Quaker Valley Middle School. Dr. Kenneth Powell became the Quaker Valley School District's first African American principal. Hired as an assistant principal in 1997, his appointment to principal came in 2002. He served Quaker Valley in an administrative capacity for over 10 years, resigning in November 2007 to accept the position of principal of the Pennsylvania Cyber Charter School, a school with a current enrollment of close to 8,000 students throughout the commonwealth of Pennsylvania.

Seven

COME ON HOME

STANLEY RIDEOUT. In 1966, a small group of black citizens of the community, spearheaded by the then director of the SCC, Stanley (Stan) Rideout, organized a homecoming event. Rideout felt that many former black Sewickleyans needed a good reason to come back home for a festive occasion and in a collective group. Rideout's selected name, "Come on Home," rather than the customary homecoming, is as unusual as the event itself. One always hears of family reunions, class reunions, organizational reunions, and church reunions. But how often does one hear of a reunion of the community? But Come on Home beckons all neighbors—friends and family alike—to return every year the first weekend in August for a fabulous weekend.

BELL STOTTS. At the beginning, Stan Rideout and Isabel (Bell) Stotts worked together as coordinators of the four-day celebration. She is shown here between sisters Carole Brothers on her left and Jennifer "Sweetie" Sims on her right. Bettie Cole was coordinator from 1973 to 1989, when she turned the reins over to Tim Lee, who still heads the event.

CLASS PALS REUNITE. Come on Home gives classmates an excellent opportunity to see one another again. Around the mid-1980s, the Annual Class Recognition was initiated to assure that former classmates do come on home at the same time. Friends of Quaker Valley class of 1965 (identified by their maiden names) are shown here, from left to right: Donna Lee, Judy Massie, Phyllis Steele, Gee Gee Cole, Beverly Lee, Gervaise Lockhart, and Sharon Patterson.

COME ON HOME, ORIGINAL COMMITTEE. In order for an event to be kept alive and successful for over 40 years, it takes a lot of hard work and many dedicated workers. The Come on Home Committee has always been at the helm. Shown here are committee members around 1986, from left to right, (first row) Velma Jackson, Bettie Cole, Tim Lee, Tyra Townsend, Kathy Gilchrist, and Florence Powell; (second row) Frances Carpenter, Ann Rideout, Richard Grey, Doug Jackson, and Earl Cole; (third row) Ed Grey, Walt Brannon, Stan Rideout, and James Champ. (Members not present are Dorothy Crawford and Bob [Bobby] Bransom.) Come on Home was originally sponsored by the SCC and Walter Robinson American Legion Post 450 and conducted by the Come on Home Committee.

REGISTRATION BROCHURE. Such mailings go out to all former members of the community. This brochure commemorated Come on Home's 20th anniversary.

A FAMILY AFFAIR BOAT RIDE. The Thursday night boat ride was always a winner, even with variations. At times it was a welcome home family boat ride where people brought their food and children. At other times, it was an adult boat ride with a buffet. Pictured here is Thaddeus "Cookie" Cook (far right) joining brother and sister Ernie Robinson and Coretha Robinson Hill and their spouses and children and their aunt Betty Robinson Jones on the 1984 boat ride.

BOAT RIDE WELCOMING COMMITTEE. Ever since the boat ride started, Come on Home originator Stan Rideout has personally welcomed everyone on the boat ride (the weekend's first event) with a hug, kiss, or handshake. Right there with him has always been Harold Parker, a charter committee member, later joined by coordinator Tim Lee, both shown here.

ELLIS "PIGGY" WILLIAMS. Every year, for decades, Ellis "Piggy" Williams (far right) made sure he got boat ride tickets for his incoming family. For years the boat ride was so popular it was fast sold out, and people had to get their tickets early. Shown here around 1990 with Piggy Williams are his daughters Marilyn Williams Worothy, Bennie Jenkins, and Gayle Vander Straaten.

ALL ABOARD, RAYMOND BUTLER AND FAMILY. Sewickley native Raymond Butler never missed a Come on Home weekend until 2006, when he was unable to travel because of illness. And most importantly, he brought his children who grew up with the tradition—the necessary ingredient for keeping the Come on Home tradition alive and well. They are shown here with him on the 1992 boat ride. From left to right are DeMark, Pamela "Wuz", Rhett, Patti, and Bonnie.

HARRY AND FRANCES BARBER CARPENTER CHILDREN. Traveling from afar to be with their parents and friends and seldom missing a Come on Home are the Carpenters. Pictured here on the boat ride (around the 1980s or 1990s) are Darlene Palmer, Kevin, and Harry Jr. and son with cousin Pamela Barber Butler.

CHECKING THE COURSE. Pictured here are Bettie Cole and a Gateway Clipper Partyline boat officer. The Osborne Coast Guard dock was the pickup and unloading spot for many years. Later they used the Sewickley Chestnut Street Culvert. The boat journeyed toward Pittsburgh to the Point where all, especially the out-of-towners, marveled at the spectacular night view of Pittsburgh all lit up in brilliant array, the fountain magnificent against the background of new buildings and skyline.

AT THE LEGION. On Fridays, Come on Home was always an open day when several different activities and events were presented. Some were a night at the races at Waterford Park, Las Vegas and Monte Carlo nights, and an old-fashioned fish fry and barbecue. But for the past several years, there has been Friday night bowling at the Jimmy Maggs Bowling Lanes, chaired by Sharon Patterson. Following is the gathering at the American Legion for karaoke night, and for more fun, dancing, eating, and greeting old friends.

KIDS FEST AT THE CENTER. Making sure the local and visiting youngsters had a good time, a Kids Fest was held on Friday afternoons for several years. It was in conjunction with the community center children's summer program.

COME ON HOME GOLF OUTING, 1985. The golf outing, getting underway early Saturday mornings, was started in 1976 by local golf enthusiast Earl Cole. Bob (Bobby) Bransom joined him, and together they cochaired the poplar event for several years. When Bransom quit—to man the bowling outing, which he initiated—Viki Rideout and Earl Cole teamed up and together ran many years of successful outings. Later others were in charge. The outings were usually held at the Black Hawk Course. Posed ready for play (from left to right) are chairperson Earl Cole, Coraopolis police chief Howard White, Judge Henry Smith of Pittsburgh, and cochairperson Bobby Bransom.

COME ON HOME CABARET DANCE. The Come on Home dance/cabaret is the centerpiece of the weekend. And it has truly been presented and celebrated in various forms and venues but always goes back to the favorite—Walter Robinson American Legion Post 450 Pavilion. And when folks are there dancing and eating and meeting and greeting one another, well, they know they are truly back home. In the beginning, and for many years, the community center ladies' guild, headed by Bell Stotts, hosted the cabaret and selected the themes and decorated accordingly. They went to great lengths decorating the pavilion to the nines. Since those early years, many different people have volunteered to keep up that spectacular tradition.

CABARET. For years, the Post 450 Pavilion could hardly hold the huge crowd that flocked to the cabaret dance. They came early to get their tables. They brought lots of family, food, and drinks—it has always been a "BYOL" (bring your own liquor) event. Pittsburgh musician Bill Gambrell and his combo provided the music for many years. (In time, other fine musicians set the pace for the evening of dancing.) It was like a big community party, and a good time was had by all. It was a time when formal family pictures were taken.

TUCKER FAMILY, c. 1985. Included in this Tucker family photograph are Addie Tucker Hayes, Bill and Carolyn Mossett Wright, Blanche Tucker Lee, James "Spike" and Sylvia Lee, Tim and Debbie Lee, and George and Louise Thomson. Within a few years, Tim would become coordinator of this fabulous weekend.

BUTLER FAMILY. Included here are Dorothy and Charles Butler, Virginia "Jennie" Butler Braxton, Juanita "Bootsie" Butler Thomas, and Harry and Laura "Snookie" Butler Vaughter with their aunt Irma Butler.

LEE FAMILY. Pictured from left to right are (first row) Hattie Lee Cole, Grace Brown Lee, their aunt Pearl Johnson Lee, and Bettie King Cole; (second row) Stanley and Mary C. "Mickey" Lee Patrick, Jane Lee Murchinson, Ray and Lynn Lee, John D. Cole, Catherine King Killins, Floyd E. Lee, Emily Lee Millen, and Pattie Killins.

BRANNON FAMILY. Walter (Walt) Brannon (on far right) has been an active member of the Come on Home Committee almost since it began. Included with him here are his wife, Laura, his brother Kenneth and his wife Alma, and Henry and Lynette Scales.

COTTOM/KIRK FAMILY. These members of the Cottom/Kirk family are dressed and ready for the August 1977 Come on Home ball. Ever since then, members of this large pioneer family have been pouring in from all over the country to partake in this annual celebration. Just a few are pictured here with the three matriarchs in the front: (from left to right) Mary Cottom Davis, Julia Cottom, and Rosa Kirk. Behind them are Ed and Mary Grey and their children Edgar Jr., Patti, and Terri; Geraldine and Aurleius Law; and Omar and Tom Owens.

COORDINATORS OFFERING AWARDS. The cabaret also has included special segments usually during intermission. Perhaps the most prestigious is the presentation of the annual Come On Home honorees who are selected each year for their outstanding support of the Come on Home weekend and its activities. On this occasion, Tim Lee and Bettie Cole bestow special honors to Stan Rideout, who started it all. Looking on are his brother Harry Rideout and Harold Parker, both longtime, hardworking committee workers.

EDNA COTTOM. Pictured here with her family is Edna Cottom, the first Come on Home honoree, honored especially for making sure that literally dozens of her family and relatives consistently attended Come on Home. Since then, the honor has been bestowed mainly upon those who have traveled yearly to attend Come On Home and its festive events.

SINGING THE COME ON HOME SONG. The highlight of the evening is the singing of the official Come on Home song (done to the tune of "Hello, Dolly!" which was popular at the time Bell Stotts and some of her ladies' guild members quickly penned their version and introduced it during intermission many years ago). It became an instant hit and has been sung at intermission ever since, before and during the grand march when all join in and greet one another.

SUNDAY WORSHIP SERVICE. All are encouraged to attend their family or former church, sit in their favorite family pews, and worship with family and friends. In 1983, Rev. E. Leroy Green Jr. of Ann Arbor, Michigan, returned to his hometown to preach at Triumph Baptist, his father's former church. Pictured with him (holding the Bible) are childhood buddies, from left to right, John Barber, Mitch Higginbotham, and Ken Whitlock.

TENNIS OUTING. Taking a break between matches are, from left to right, Al Zigler, Walt Smith, Ike Davis, Ed Grey, and Stan Rideout. Ed Grey, a tennis enthusiast for most all his life, was instrumental in initiating and conducting the tennis outing, which usually was held on the center tennis court. Refreshments were furnished for the players. Members of the Riverview Tennis Club of Pittsburgh were regulars. In time, there was an increase in tennis players and an occasional change of venue. Below, a sizeable group of players takes time to pose at the academy courts.

FAMILY FUN DAY. Sunday Family Fun Day or Farewell Day (as it was often referred to) was held on the community center grounds and the athletic field and Post 450 grounds. Events included a family swim (after the pool was completed in 1972), a tennis outing, softball games, outdoor basketball games, competitive games and contests for children and adults, miniature carnivals, live music, disco music, cookouts, picnics, and refreshments for sale. The proximity of the community center, the athletic field, and Post 450 located at the foot of Chadwick Street was ideal and nostalgic for the Sewickley Valley Come on Home setting.

NO PLACE LIKE HOME. A sentiment shared by many, descendants of the pioneer Solomon Toliver family are elated to come home for a joyous occasion like Come on Home. Pictured here are Lou Ella Toliver Pendleton and her nephew Clarence Craft and his wife, Janet.

FAMILY PICTURE. Pictured are brothers and cousins Moses "Tish" Snead, Ethel and Roger Snead, Bobby Higginbotham, and Ada L. Smith, happy to be together again at Come on Home and enjoying the events. Along with the traditional, there have been many other types of activities throughout the 40 years, including welcome home and get acquainted cocktail parties, Saturday afternoon card party tournaments, Sunday champagne brunches, and Post 450 drill team reunions.

A Tradition Since 1903

Sewickley Herald

...ing Aleppo, Bell Acres, Edgeworth, Glenfield, Haysville, Leet, Leetsdale, Osborne, Sewickley, Sewickley Heights, Sewickley...

Thursday, August 10, 2006   Volume 103,

SIDE

EMPO

...the Child Health
...Sewickley work all
...re children receive
...o learn more about
...e Page 13.

ND ABOUT

...aspberries,
...and
...d Hill
...n, no
...un-
...Page
...t for the season.

ORTS

...soar as sports
...ach for high school
...Page 33.

NDEX

...s 2
.............................6
........................13
........................30
...wn...............29
.....................33
...te................37

97 53440 6

CABARET

Friends, family Come On Home

IT WAS a great weekend to reunite at the annual Come On Home event. Above, (front) Darla Adams, Valerie Smith, Steve Parish, Beth Kennedy, Stanley Kennedy, (back) James Adams and Frankie Smith enjoy the cabaret at American Legion Post 450. At right, Hallie Pace, Walt Brannon, Stan and Ann Rideout, Henry Scales, Robert Norman, Darlene Barnes, Tim Lee and Linda Whitlock spend the day together.

Photo by Todd Brunozzi

SAFE...

AED he
firefigh
stay sa

By Kristina Kregie...
Staff writer

The Cochr...
Company receive...
on lesson on how...
when a trainee...
during a first-aid...
class held earlier...
conjunction with...
certification.

Worried that h...
ing a heart att...
medics rushed th...
to Sewickley Valle...

Though it was...
mined that the...
fered a panic...
scare prompted...
ment to look into...
a life-saving devic...
another emergenc...

An automate...
difibrillator (AE...
portable electro...
used to diagnose...
sudden cardiac...
using an electric s...
a heartbeat back...
rect rhythm. Th...
relatively simple...
minimal training...
proof—it can't s...
one who doesn't n...

Jeff Neff, fire...
the department a...
state grant to p...
device, but did n...
thing back reg...
funding. They the...
solicit local bus...
donations to help...
new AED).

In late spring...
Sam Bruno ran...
Fecko of David...
Insurance (MPF...
Inc.) on Broad...
him about the i...

Continue...

Visit us online at www.yoursewickley.com

CURRENT COME ON HOME COMMITTEE. Stan Rideout's vision became a reality. People love it. They have come back home by the droves. And the hometown folks and the Come on Home Committee throughout the years have gone out of their way to receive and welcome them. All of which speaks eloquently of their love for their Sewickley Valley hometown. Kudos to the current members of the Come on Home Committee; they are responsible for keeping it alive and well after all these years. Shown in this *Sewickley Herald* news clipping from left to right are Hallie Pace, Walt Brannon, Stan Rideout, Ann Rideout, Henry Scales (current Post 450 commander), Robert Norman, Darlene Barnes, Tim Lee, and Linda Whitlock. (Courtesy of the Sewickley Herald.)

JOHN TURNER. John Turner, a memorable aged pioneer of Sewickley Valley, greets participants of the Come on Home boat ride in the early 1970s. He also bows slightly, tilts his head, doffs his cap, and bids "Adieu!"

COME ON HOME, SMOOTH SAILING. Since most of the old-timers are gone, it is up to the following generations to keep the spirit and the magic of Come on Home alive, which originator Stan Rideout always sums up as, "See people greet each other who haven't seen each other in many years."

BIBLIOGRAPHY

Blockson, Charles. *The Underground Railroad in Pennsylvania*. Jacksonville, NC: Flame International, 1981.

Cole, Bettie. "African Americans in the Sewickley Valley." *Sewickley Sesquicentennial*, 1990, 28–30.

———. *Their Story: The History of Blacks/African Americans in Sewickley and Edgeworth*. Sewickley, PA: self-published, 2000.

———. "Ladies Guild." *"Carnival" 20th Anniversary Come on Home Weekend*, 1986, 15.

Ellis, A. L. *Lights and Shadows of Sewickley Life or Memories of Sweet Valley*. Philadelphia: J. B. Lippincott Company, 1893.

Nevin, F. T. *The Village of Sewickley*. Sewickley, PA: The Sewickley Printing Shop, 1929.

Sewickley Valley Historical Society. *Sewickley*. Charleston, SC: Arcadia Publishing, 2006.

Shields, B. G., ed. *Sewickley Up Front and Personal: A Decade in Black and White; Covers from the 1970s Sewickley Herald*. 2003.

Switala, W. J. *Underground Railroad*. Mechanicsburg, PA: Stackpole Books, 2001.

Tresle Board (anniversary issue) 3, no. 1 (January–February 1970).

Whitlock, K., and K. Burgess. *Breaking Barriers: The Ken Whitlock Story*. Gibsonia, PA: Kenneth Whitlock, 2001.

Visit us at
arcadiapublishing.com

www.ingramcontent.com/pod-product-compliance
Lightning Source LLC
Chambersburg PA
CBHW080546110426
42813CB00006B/1224